A
BRAVE
FACE

A
BRAVE
FACE

TWO CULTURES, TWO FAMILIES, AND THE
IRAQI GIRL WHO BOUND THEM TOGETHER

BARBARA MARLOWE AND
TEEBA FURAT MARLOWE
WITH JENNIFER KEIRN

W PUBLISHING GROUP

AN IMPRINT OF THOMAS NELSON

Published in Nashville, Tennessee, by W Publishing, an imprint of Thomas Nelson.

Thomas Nelson titles may be purchased in bulk for educational, business, fund-raising, or sales promotional use. For information, please e-mail SpecialMarkets@ThomasNelson.com.

Scripture quotations are taken from the Holy Bible, New International Version®, NIV®. Copyright © 1973, 1978, 1984, 2011 by Biblica, Inc.® Used by permission of Zondervan. All rights reserved worldwide. www.Zondervan.com. The "NIV" and "New International Version" are trademarks registered in the United States Patent and Trademark Office by Biblica, Inc.®

Any Internet addresses, phone numbers, or company or product information printed in this book are offered as a resource and are not intended in any way to be or to imply an endorsement by Thomas Nelson, nor does Thomas Nelson vouch for the existence, content, or services of these sites, phone numbers, companies, or products beyond the life of this book.

ISBN 978-0-7852-2136-4 (HC)
ISBN 978-0-7852-2145-6 (SC)
ISBN 978-0-7852-2139-5 (eBook)

Library of Congress Control Number: 2018954916

From Teeba: I dedicate my story to my brother Yousif—a beautiful guardian angel who is the epitome of undying love and an everlasting faith in our one and only God.

From Dunia: I dedicate this book to all who have helped Teeba face the challenges of her hardships, and for the hope and strength that made her dark life bright. And to the most loving mother ever, the queen of moms, the greatest Barbara.

From Barbara: I dedicate this book to my mother, Jean, and to Teeba's brother Yousif—who "sent her to me to be my daughter." And to Dunia, the most courageous woman I know.

We delight in the beauty of the butterfly, but rarely admit the changes it has gone through to achieve that beauty.

—MAYA ANGELOU

CONTENTS

CONTENTS

CHAPTER 1

EYES WIDE OPEN

What mesmerized me at first were Teeba's eyes.

They were dark, round, and soulful. The eyes of a child who'd seen more than she should have in her short life. They were surrounded by burned and mottled skin, thick with scar tissue, covering what should have been warm, smooth, olive skin. The scar tissue traveled up her forehead and across much of her scalp. All that remained of her dark hair was a few wisps just over her right eye, above her ears, and scattered in the back of her head. Clad in a plaid jumper zipped up tight to her neck, she was seated on her father's lap, her tiny body tucked into his, with his protective hand clutching her shoulder.

She was four years old, living thousands of miles away in war-torn Iraq. But as I gazed into her eyes through the black-and-white photo in my Sunday newspaper, I felt as though she were sitting right there in front of me.

In an instant, it was as if the air had been sucked out of the room, taking with it everything happening around me. The sun streaming through my window on that July morning, the sounds of my husband, Tim, heading out to walk our dog, Phantom, the smell of the hot coffee I'd just poured—it all faded away.

Through the lens of the camera, the little girl's eyes locked with mine, imploring: *Help me.*

I'd only intended a quick flip through the newspaper before Tim and I headed out for a round of golf. That was how we often spent our weekend days in the summer. We were empty-nesters, me in my early fifties and he in his sixties, me childless and he with three grown children from a previous marriage.

But the eyes of four-year-old Teeba brought me to a dead stop on page A3 of the July 16, 2006, issue of Cleveland's *The Plain Dealer.*

Her picture appeared beside an article headlined, "War's Scars Leave Dozens of Iraqis in Pain, Despair: Not Enough Surgeons to Fix Terrible Injuries." As I read the article, I learned Teeba had been riding in a taxi with her father and brother in one of the most dangerous regions of Iraq, Diyala Province, about sixty miles north of the Iraqi capital of Baghdad, when the vehicle was struck by a roadside bomb. She was just nineteen months old. Thankfully, Teeba was wearing a heavy coat that protected most of her body from the flames, but her hands, face, ears, and scalp were severely burned, leaving her disfigured. Her father was uninjured, but her three-year-old brother, Yousif, later died from his injuries.

Teeba was just one of the many Iraqis at that time who had suffered disfiguring injuries due to violence but were left without good options for proper medical care. According to the article, the Iraqi Assembly for Plastic Surgeons estimated that twenty of the thirty-four plastic surgeons registered there before the 2003 invasion had been killed or had fled due to threats of violence. Those remaining were bogged down by heavy caseloads and shortages of supplies and equipment. The waiting list for even an examination by plastic surgeons at Baghdad's government-run hospital was at least a year.

To be honest, I normally wouldn't have done anything more than skim the headline on such an article during those days. Even though our country was more than three years into the Iraq War, I really didn't pay much attention to the war or Middle East politics. I was like a lot of Americans who hear the day-in, day-out stories of horrific violence but allow it to fade into the background of our lives. I'd just skim the headlines before getting back to the daily rhythms of my life.

That's why I'd missed some startling events in the weeks prior to that Sunday. A suicide truck bomb had killed more than sixty people in a Baghdad market. A bus carrying mourners returning from the burial of a loved one was ambushed, and thirty people at a meeting of the Olympic Committee had been abducted. On the same day I first saw Teeba's picture, the death count of American service members reached 2,539, and Iraq was on the verge of outright civil war.

Sixty people dead, thirty people kidnapped, and the 2,539th soldier killed. Back then, those were all just numbers to me—sound bites that had been going in one ear and out the other for years.

Until that day.

Seeing Teeba was like a slap in the face. Suddenly I was staring into the eyes of one little girl who put a human face on the stream of bad news coming out of Iraq. There was one quote from the article in particular that gave me a good, hard shake, making me decide to do something. From the caption of Teeba's photo, I read this quote from her father, Furat: "She's already asked about getting a wig."

A wig, I thought. *Maybe I can get her a wig.*

Only a few months prior, I'd co-chaired a fund-raising event for Wigs for Kids, a nonprofit organization that makes custom human-hair wigs for kids who have lost their hair due to illness or injury. Sitting on my work to-do list at that moment were a bunch of follow-up tasks still lingering from the Wigs for Kids fund-raiser, so it was still fresh in my mind.

I grabbed scissors from the kitchen drawer and, without taking my eyes off Teeba's face, I clipped out the article, headed upstairs to my home office, and made a photocopy. I taped the original to the wall over my desk, and I folded up the copy and placed it in the pocket of my golf jacket. At that moment I knew I wouldn't stop until I found her, no matter how long it took. I felt a steely determination that was different from anything I'd experienced in the past, even with my trademark laser focus.

I was still staring into Teeba's eyes, and I realized I was crying. *Help me*, her eyes begged.

I will.

I hadn't wanted to help with the Wigs for Kids event to begin with. It violated my number-one rule of volunteer work: no kids. I'd never been able to have my own children, and the thought of getting involved with a children's charity was just too painful.

I always expected that I would have children. When I was growing up in the 1970s, plenty of the teenagers around me were experimenting with hard drugs, but I resisted, fearful it would cause birth defects in the children I was sure I would have one day.

I met my first husband when I was nineteen. The signs of trouble were there before we got married. At one point I split up with him and moved to Chicago, seeking a fresh start on my own. But when he would come to visit, he seemed to have changed his ways. So when I decided to come back to Cleveland to marry him when I was twenty-five and he was forty-one, I thought things would be different. I ignored everything and everyone warning me.

In the beginning, he shut the door on having children. Later he opened the door just a tiny bit by telling me "maybe." Our marriage crashed and burned after five years, when I was only thirty years old and knew for sure that my priorities were not his. I asked myself: *If I had a friend in this situation, what advice would I give her?* I would tell her that she should leave, and I knew I needed to take my own advice. And I never looked back.

I started seeing Tim soon after my separation, and he had all the attributes of the guy I'd always dreamed of being with. He was a dedicated father to his three children, always treated people kindly and with respect, and had a crazy sense of humor that I loved. He was a man whose glass was always half-full, with a sense of calmness and control about him. I thought again of the kind of advice I would have given a friend—*This is a good guy, now don't blow it!*

But when we married in 1988, he was forty-five, his children were six, eleven, and twelve, and he didn't want more. I could see the door swinging shut on my dream of becoming a mother. Soon after we married, the bleeding started—intense pain and hemorrhaging that led to a diagnosis of uterine fibroids, with hysterectomy as the recommended treatment.

Then that was it. The door closed and locked. I would never be a mother.

On the outside, I hid behind the bravado of a career woman who didn't have time for kids and the burdens that came along with motherhood. Few people knew how I really felt. That's why I'd always adhered to that "no kids" rule in my volunteer work. It brought me too close to that secret pain that I'd tried so hard to hide. Most of my energy went into helping charities serving animals in need. But my good friend Maria Dietz, who worked at a hair salon and spa and had volunteered with Wigs for Kids in the past, pulled me into the planning process for the event, even though I resisted.

It was a bread crumb, I see now—one of those tiny seeds God plants in your life when He's planning to take you in a whole different direction than what you had in mind.

A wig. I can get a wig for Teeba.

Teeba was the first thing on my mind when I woke up the next morning. I headed to my desk in my home office, where I launched into my work as a marketing and public relations consultant. I was finishing the wrap-up from the Wigs for Kids fund-raiser and digging into a new marketing project for one of my largest clients.

But the article about Teeba, staring down at me from the wall above my desk, kept distracting me. Finally, I set aside what I'd been working on and instead began searching online for contact information for James

Palmer, the reporter who'd written the article about Teeba. It didn't take long to dig up his email address.

Just before 10:00 a.m. on July 17, 2006, I typed the email that would change my life forever:

> Hi James—
>
> Re: Teeba Furat, 4-year-old girl who survived bombing in Iraq
>
> I can get this little girl a wig. I'm affiliated with Wigs for Kids. Please call me asap if you can.
>
> Barbara Marlowe

I clicked Send. Then I started working the phones.

CHAPTER 2

A BOY AND HIS BIKE

It would be years before I finally pieced together everything that happened to Teeba and her family on November 29, 2003. I learned that Teeba's older brother, three-year-old Yousif, had been enviously watching the other kids in their rural village riding their bicycles, and he'd begged their father, Furat, to let him have a bike of his own.

Violence was a daily part of their lives, so they didn't leave the village often. But on that day, Furat told Yousif that he would take him to look at bicycles once he and Teeba had visited the doctor and finished their shopping in Baqubah, about fifteen minutes away. I can just picture Yousif's squirming impatience—a typical three-year-old stuck running errands with his dad while dreaming about the possibility of getting his own bike. Furat called for a taxi to take his two children and himself on their errands, and he sat in front with the driver while Yousif and Teeba climbed into the back. By November, temperatures have usually cooled into the sixties in that part of Iraq, and Teeba wore a heavy overcoat, a choice I would clearly see as fortunate later on.

The trip was short, but it was dangerous. People in Iraq had been hopeful about what Saddam Hussein's fall from power that April would mean for their country, but the summer and fall of 2003 had been bloody seasons. Terrorist groups like Al-Qaeda were gaining strength, and guerrilla warfare was tearing apart cities and villages like theirs. Just a few months before, a suicide bomber exploded close to the United Nations headquarters in Baghdad, killing seventeen and wounding more than one hundred, the deadliest attack in UN history. Improvised explosive devices (IEDs) littered Iraq's streets.

It could have been anything—a dead animal or a bag of trash or even just a carefully hidden mound of earth. Concealed there, the roadside bomb waited for Furat and his children to come along, and when their taxi hit it, the back seat was immediately consumed by flames. Teeba's coat protected most of her body from the fire, but her head, face, and hands were scorched, resulting in third-degree burns. The cartilage of her ears was burned off, and much of her scalp was burned severely enough to ensure she would never grow hair again. Furat was uninjured. Yousif survived, but he died shortly thereafter as he was transported to a government-run hospital.

I cringe when I imagine the medical care Teeba received when she reached the hospital, which lacked the basic supplies and skilled healthcare providers she urgently needed. Nurses further damaged her skin by scrubbing it with water. A full three days passed before Furat was able to transfer Teeba to an American Red Cross burn clinic in Baghdad, where she finally received dry powder and ointments to treat her burns. After forty days in the burn clinic, Teeba was permitted to return to her village.

As devastating as I imagined her recovery was when I heard about it, my heart broke at the life that awaited Teeba in her village as she healed and grew. There were people in her community who weren't supportive of those with disabilities and disfigurements, and she was shunned for her appearance. Children teased her to the point where her parents worried about how she would be treated when she started school. And the possibilities that she could one day marry or live independently were slim. After the pain of losing their firstborn son, Furat and his wife, Dunia, then had to struggle to find the money to pay for Teeba's medications, which were little more than salves to help in her healing and ease the intense itching. The kind of intensive plastic surgery that would be required to repair her scarred face and scalp was out of reach.

Then they met James Palmer. He was working as a freelance journalist in Iraq at the time, and he learned of Teeba's story through an employee at a Baghdad blood bank. That employee didn't know much about Teeba, only that she was a young girl who'd been injured in a roadside bombing. But he told me that tidbit stuck in his memory, and when he later decided to pursue a story about Iraqi civilians, both children and adults, who had been severely injured in attacks and were struggling to receive the care they needed, he thought about Teeba.

So James invited Furat and Teeba, by then four years old, to come to his hotel in Baghdad for an interview. Nearly three years had passed since Teeba's accident, and the violence in Iraq had continued to escalate. I would only later come to understand the level of crisis the country faced at that time. Earlier that year, the al-Askari mosque in Samarra, one of the most revered Shiite shrines in Iraq, had been bombed. That event touched off a wave of sectarian violence between Shiite and Sunni Muslims, two sects of the Islamic faith who have been deeply divided for more than a thousand years. On the day of the Samarra mosque bombing, mobs took to the streets in cities throughout Iraq, calling for revenge and setting fire to dozens of Sunni mosques as retaliation. In a single day, Shiite militia had attacked twenty-seven Sunni mosques in Baghdad alone. The tensions in the city had only escalated since then.

It would be a dangerous trip for Furat and Teeba, but it was the only possible way they could meet James. As a freelance journalist, he told me he had a hard time paying translators enough to accompany him on a trip as treacherous as the one to their village would have been. He also couldn't afford security. To get around, James and the young, inexperienced translators he was able to afford were forced to roam the city in a beat-up car trying to pass James off as an Iraqi so he could do his reporting.

As dangerous as that trip to Baghdad would be, Furat wasn't deterred. He was so desperate to get help for Teeba that he agreed to bring her the sixty miles by bus to meet James in his Baghdad hotel room on June 5, 2006.

James's hotel was located in the upper-middle-class Baghdad district of Karrada, partially obscured from the road by trees and with a porch outside that was usually buried in dust. When Furat and Teeba arrived at James's door, Teeba was initially shy, a tiny figure hiding behind her father. In contrast, James told me that Furat was warm and friendly, with a big smile and easy laugh. James often kept the shades drawn across the large picture window to block out the glaring summer sun, and in the darkened room Furat found a *Tom and Jerry* cartoon Teeba could watch on TV while they talked.

Through James's translator, Furat began to tell their story—the accident, Yousif's death, Teeba's long recovery, and their struggles to pay her medical bills. Kids ridiculed her, adults stared, and Teeba was jealous of other children who had hair and unblemished skin.

"She's supposed to start school next year," said Furat. "I worry about how she'll be treated by the other children."

Just like many other families that James was interviewing at the time, Furat told him how frustrated he was with the Iraqi hospital system.

"They can't do anything for her here," Furat said. "She's already asked about getting a wig, but I'm hoping for more. I'm hoping there's a way we can find medical treatment for her burns."

"I can't promise that my story will do anything to help Teeba," cautioned James. "In fact, most of the time nothing results from stories like these."

"I understand," said Furat. "I would sell everything I own in order to take care of her."

Like a typical four-year-old, Teeba quickly got restless and anxious to leave. She was also antsy because she needed to use the bathroom, but was afraid to use the Western-style toilets in James's hotel room. But before their conversation ended, James asked if he could take some photos of Teeba. Furat called her over from her cartoons and she climbed up on his lap, wearing an orange plaid dress with her scarred head uncovered. Then

James took the photo that Furat hoped would help grant Teeba's wish and make his dream come true. The shot captured her imploring eyes, staring deep into the camera, which I would see in the newspaper just over a month later.

After the interview, James, Furat, and Teeba went outdoors and had a lunch of kebabs and sodas in an outdoor restaurant, where little Teeba was finally able to use a restroom. As they said their goodbyes, James reminded Furat again that it was highly unlikely that his article would result in any help for Teeba.

In fact, it would probably take a miracle.

CHAPTER 3

TEEBA: TEARS
OF A CHILD

M y mom called me Teeba—which means "good" or "sweet"—because she says when I was born after a long and complicated birth, I smiled at her. Life as an infant in a small, war-torn Iraqi village was truly devastating before and after the accident. From stories I've heard, I was something close to a little Arab Curious George. Every story my mother tells me ends with me getting myself into some kind of trouble.

She says I used to chase snakes, catch butterflies, and run into secret gardens before I could barely speak full sentences. The snakes would bury themselves in the sand, and my sister and I would chase them. The sand is funny like that—it hides every creature, then brings them to the surface when you least expect it. One day I ran into the house crying that a butterfly stung me. I had actually been trying to catch a bee. My mom tells me stories of when she used to carry me under the long black cloak that covered her body, known as an abaya, to protect me—how she'd take me to the market or even the mosque to pray. I have only the vaguest memory of the mosque we used to visit regularly. It was a dome with intricate detailing and calligraphy laced on its holy walls.

Since I was only nineteen months old at the time of the bombing, I don't remember too much of the incident itself. But one thing I seem to recall is the way everything happened in slow motion. Every second was extended to a long, painful, suffocating minute.

It seemed we were swept away by a huge force in the air. I could see nothing, but the screams of the villagers will never escape my memory. I remember the sorrowful yells. I heard no words, just agony in trembling voices. After what seemed an eternity, I awoke without eyesight on a hospital bed. So, I missed a huge gap of the story—maybe I lost consciousness, maybe I was too young to know everything that took place, or maybe I haven't let myself remember something so miserable and heartbreaking for my own sake.

While in the hospital, I only remember being in pain and unaware of my surroundings due to the loss of my eyesight. For a long time afterward I would often wake up unable to breathe, struggling to pull away from nightmares of those days.

Many of my memories from that hospital bed are sad. Such as my parents and relatives crying at the loss of my innocent brother, or their cries of guilt as they saw me in such pain. My mother says the doctors told her that even though I would survive, it would be better for me to die an honorable death—because no one would ever love me with all of the burns on my face and body.

The only happy occasion I'm aware of from my time in the hospital is a story my mom told me recently. She says the family gathered at my bedside as they awaited the doctors' reassurance that I would regain my eyesight. After hours of waiting for what they hoped would be good news, the doctor came out to update the room. When he told them my eyes were perfect and would go back to normal, the family cheered for hours. My dad and uncles played the banjo, drums, and even brought a radio to celebrate.

Mom also said that was the first time I ever danced. There we were in a crowded little room, me dancing on a cheap hospital bed, unable to see, with my family members playing music and cheering while the ladies sang and danced around the room. This is one of my favorite stories from the past, because my mom always tells it to me with a happy smile on her face.

I like to see her smile.

CHAPTER 4

THE SEARCH BEGINS

I didn't even wait for James Palmer's response before immediately shooting off emails and making calls to everyone I could think of who might be able to help Teeba.

The first person I called was Jeffrey Paul, the founder of Wigs for Kids. Jeffrey was a hair stylist, and he started Wigs for Kids thirty-five years ago to provide wigs made of real hair free of charge to kids suffering from all sorts of hair loss.

"You're not going to believe the irony of this," I began when Jeffrey picked up the phone. "What are the chances that just as I was finishing work on your Wigs for Kids event, I would read about a little girl on the other side of the world who wants nothing more than her own wig?"

I ran through everything I knew about Teeba while he listened carefully.

"So can you help?" I asked him.

"Of course I can help," Jeffery responded. "You'll just have to get someone in Iraq to take very careful measurements of her head, then we can have the wig made exactly to her specifications and ship it to her."

It seemed so simple. It should have felt like a first victory in my mission to help this little girl. But as I thanked him and hung up, I was already starting to realize the flaws in my plan.

Who would take the measurements? How could I be sure that person would follow the precise instructions despite the language barrier? Could it be shipped there safely? And how much would the shipping cost? What if the size wasn't right? Or the color? Plus, she was still growing. A wig we made then probably wouldn't fit in another year or two. There was too much room for error.

Within minutes of my conversation with Jeffrey, I was already formulating a new plan in my mind. Maybe just getting her a wig isn't thinking big enough. The article said only that Teeba was asking for a wig, but maybe her family would like for her to get medical treatment in the United States. Maybe I could get her here to Cleveland to get reconstructive surgery for her scars.

Now, many people would come to this moment, realize they were treading into water that was way over their heads, and turn back to higher ground. And in this case, the water wouldn't just be deep, it would be a rushing tide that could sweep me into challenges I couldn't possibly anticipate. But I've never been the kind of person who stops when I see deep, rushing water ahead of me. Instead, I look for the stepping stones that will take me across. Even when I can't see the stepping stones, sometimes I leap anyway, confident that one will appear.

To me, the stepping stones were so clearly lined up that this mission seemed meant to be.

Teeba needs a wig. Check! I knew Jeffrey Paul and was a volunteer for Wigs for Kids.

Teeba needs medical treatment. Check! My dear friend Loree Vick had just taken a job as director of media and public relations at University Hospitals in Cleveland, which has an amazing, award-winning pediatric hospital, Rainbow Babies & Children's Hospital.

I need to get the word out so others will help her. Check! After a thirty-year career in PR, I had great contacts among local media outlets.

Everyone who knows me has seen me latch onto a project and become completely consumed by it. Hearing the word *no* has never been a barrier to me. I just dart around it and keep barreling ahead.

But helping Teeba wasn't just another one of my projects. Seeing her face and hearing her story had captured my heart, and I couldn't just let the image of Teeba's sweet face fade into memory while I continued on with my life. That photograph and her penetrating eyes kept me determined, and I never once considered turning back.

Never.

My next call was to Loree, to ask for advice about getting the hospital to donate treatment. She was a relatively new employee of University Hospitals, so she couldn't make a commitment that the hospital would help, but she at least promised to get the conversation started.

Just a few hours later, James Palmer responded to my email and offered to talk more, so I dashed off a response outlining my new plan:

From: Barbara Marlowe
To: James Palmer

I am affiliated with Rainbow Babies & Children's Hospital in Cleveland, Ohio. Can we get this little girl here, to perhaps treat her for these burns and scars? And I also do fund-raising for Wigs for Kids, a nonprofit, international organization started here in Cleveland that provides wigs for children with cancer, alopecia, and burns. I contacted the founder and he would be happy to create a wig for this child. These wigs will not fall off; the kids can play, swim, do whatever they do. I would sure like to help this little girl. Her picture devastated me. Maybe we can help others in the process too.

Barbara

As the week wore on, the emails were flying back and forth between me, James, Loree, and her colleagues at Rainbow Babies & Children's Hospital. Loree was able to convince the hospital's administrators to talk with me about Teeba's case.

From: Barbara Marlowe
To: James Palmer, Loree Vick

If you folks give me the direction, I will do the legwork. Thank you—I'd really like to get the ball rolling for her, I'm sure the red tape could be a potential problem, and I'm sure sooner is better to get her help, rather than later. GOD BLESS YOU ALL!!!!

Barbara

While James worked on his end to make contact with Teeba's family and give me contact information for government officials there who could help with visas to enter the United States, I continued to call everyone I could think of to solicit their help. I believed that my drive to help this little girl from Iraq would be met with others feeling compelled to do the same.

How could anyone say no? I thought. How could they not want to help her? How could they not want to help me make this possible for her?

I stood in front of the mirror in my bedroom, trying on and rejecting outfit after outfit, finally settling on my favorite blue suit and cream silk blouse. Call me old school, but I always dress my best when I have to ask someone to help me. It shows how seriously I'm taking something, which I hope will make them feel the same way.

Loree had managed to get me a meeting with Dr. Avroy Fanaroff, who was then the chair of the Department of Pediatrics at Rainbow Babies & Children's Hospital. This was my chance to make my appeal to the hospital to take on Teeba's case. I knew that I was making a hefty request. I was asking University Hospitals to commit to treating a patient without even seeing her, and, of course, having no idea how much it would cost.

As I drove the thirty-five minutes from my house to the hospital, I ran through my talking points. I turned over and over in my head how I could make a strong enough case to convince Dr. Fanaroff. I was feeling confident, sure that anyone who heard her story would feel as compelled as I did to help her. But at the same time I felt anxious, knowing that my ability to solicit his help in this moment would make or break Teeba's shot at getting treatment. Anxious knowing that even if they agreed to help, I still might not be able to get her into the country.

It was late afternoon when I arrived at Dr. Fanaroff's office, clutching my newspaper clipping with Teeba's photo. His secretary brought me into his office to wait while he finished his rounds. My eyes roamed the room while I waited, scanning the brightly colored photographs from his travels all around the world that covered the walls.

"Barbara?" the doctor said in a soft, melodic South African accent as he entered the room. "Hello, I'm Dr. Fanaroff." He extended his hand and enveloped mine. Dr. Fanaroff was tall, with kind eyes, a calm demeanor, white hair, and a neatly trimmed short beard. He seated himself across from me and gave me his full attention.

I thrust my newspaper clipping toward him and just spoke from my heart. I told him how Teeba's eyes grabbed me from the moment I saw them in the newspaper and how her story spoke to my soul. I told him everything I had learned about her accident and condition, which wasn't much. I told him about everything I was doing to try to get her to Cleveland and about the people who were helping me along the way.

"So," I said, coming up for air after talking nonstop for ten minutes, "can you help her?"

Dr. Fanaroff sat silently for a moment and studied Teeba's picture.

"Well, I can't commit to treatment until we see her," he said. "It's difficult to determine what would be required by just looking at a photograph. But if you can get her here, I will evaluate her."

I felt a thrill in my chest and a broad smile grew across my face. It was my first huge victory! I felt encouraged and unstoppable. The door had opened just a bit, and now I just had to kick it completely open. If I could get the hospital to agree, which was an enormous hurdle, all the rest should fall into place. Right?

I thanked Dr. Fanaroff over and over for the chance to present Teeba's case and for his time and consideration. We talked about hopefully getting an appointment for her evaluation in a few months, then on to my next big challenge—figuring out how to get Teeba here for that appointment.

I went back to working the phones. A local, private aviation company said they were willing to donate air travel, but they could only get her to Cleveland from New York or Chicago. They didn't do international flights. I asked Royal Jordanian Airlines to donate airfare, but they refused. Eventually I was able to make connections with my local congressmen to ask for help getting visas, but they told me they couldn't provide much help until Teeba's family had started the process of applying for visas there.

I had a lot of contacts at the local television stations and newspapers, so I had Teeba's story on the air and in our local papers within days. I reached out to contacts I'd established over the years at NBC's and ABC's local affiliate networks. I opened a "Help Teeba Furat" account at a local bank and got the word out to solicit donations. I contacted our local Ronald McDonald House through Rainbow Babies & Children's Hospital, which agreed to provide housing for Teeba and her family when they arrived.

Meanwhile, James had spoken with Furat, who was hopeful at the possibility of getting Teeba medical care and was willing to make the trip with his wife, Dunia, two-year-old Fatima, and their infant son, Aboody. But they were poor, and they needed passports for the youngest children and money to apply for visas, so I transferred money to James to give to Furat.

From: Barbara Marlowe

To: James Palmer

Can you find out how soon they could be ready to leave and how many would be coming? There is the potential for it happening quickly—who knows, but just to give me some sort of idea. I'm trying to make this happen quickly—but obviously obtaining the visas and getting clearance might take a bit longer. Also, I assume they speak little to no English. Any dietary restrictions???

Barbara

I want to go back and slap myself for being so naïve. Earlier I had told James the red tape might be a "potential problem," but I had no idea that a mountain of it was waiting to entangle me. The complexity of the process soon became clear: At that time, there was no US Embassy in Baghdad. After they secured passports, Teeba and her family would have to travel to the American Consulate in Amman, Jordan, more than five hundred miles from their home, to apply for the visas they would need to enter the United States. They needed money to get there and accommodations while they waited for approval. They would not be able to book flights to the United States until after their visas were approved, and no appointments at University Hospitals could be made until the flights were confirmed.

But I believe that God often puts blinders on us. If we stop to look at the long-term picture other than what's right in front of us, it all becomes too overwhelming, and we never move forward. In our case, if we truly knew what we were getting into, we likely would not have done it. I was looking down at my feet, focused only on taking the next right step. If I had stopped and looked around, I'm not sure I would have continued against the incredible obstacles and challenges that were ahead of us.

If I had to go back and give Barbara-then some advice from Barbara-now, I probably would tell her to stay naïve. In my mission to help Teeba, there was no room for hesitation. To me, it was easy to feel unstoppable because I was too naïve to think that this big goal I'd set for myself couldn't come to fruition.

So I just kept taking steps. It felt like I moved three steps backward for every one step forward, but I kept going. I put my faith in God, and I just knew it was all going to work out.

CHAPTER 5

MY BIG BREAK

Maybe I thought it would all work out, but others weren't so sure. My friends thought I was completely crazy. Tim was supportive, as always. After twenty years of marriage, he was accustomed to seeing me barreling forward at full steam, rarely coming up for air. He knew I was trying to help the little girl from Iraq I'd read about in the newspaper, but I didn't always share the details of exactly what I was up to. I kept him in the loop on the most significant developments, but there was so much happening day-to-day that it seemed too cumbersome to be updating him constantly.

I just charged ahead on my own, moving from one step to the next to help Teeba. In a career like mine, I'm used to hearing the word *no*. It's never been a sign for me to stop. My response to hearing *no* is, "I'll call again in a couple of weeks."

But even I wore down into discouragement as the elation of my initial progress faded. The process ground to a near halt because of red tape and logistical problems. Letters, emails, and calls flew back and forth between us, the hospital, the airlines, James Palmer, immigration officials here and in Jordan, and Mahmood—a relative of Teeba's who spoke English and worked for an international aid organization. I sent a smiling photograph of myself holding our dog, Phantom, and a sign with Teeba's name and a heart around it, hoping my intentions would be clear to her and her family.

Then one day, as my frustration became too much to bear, I stalked out to my driveway to get some air. Staring at the ground, I paced in a circle, angry and frustrated.

Why am I doing this? Why isn't this working out?

As my emotions built, I raised my face to the sky.

"You put me here, You put this little girl in my heart," I yelled out loud to God. "Now why aren't You helping me?"

Just a few years earlier, it wouldn't have occurred to me to ask God for help at a time like this. I wasn't a very religious person throughout most of my life. My father was Jewish and my mother was Catholic, but neither was particularly observant. I'd been baptized Catholic but never received the other sacraments.

But in 2000, something happened that ignited a desire in me to seek out a connection to God. As a middle-aged woman with no children, my dog Phantom *was* my child. This tiny five-pound white Maltese helped to fill some of the emptiness in my soul. He allowed me to be a mother in some small way.

When Phantom was two years old, as I was headed out to take him for a walk, the springs of the garage door snapped and the heavy door fell, pinning his front two legs to the ground. I screamed and ran to him, but the door was too heavy for me to lift. Tim heard me and dashed outside, manually lifting the garage door while Phantom cried and screamed too. As we raced our whimpering Phantom to the veterinary emergency clinic, I prayed to God that if He would heal Phantom and allow him to walk again, I would dedicate myself to helping other animals in need.

It's the kind of dealmaking that many people do with God in times of fear and grief. They say they'll do something in God's name—if only God would do something for them first. But Phantom's accident stirred up something in me. After that, I began to see signs of God's work in my life. I began to crave a spiritual connection in a way I never had before. Before that, I'd simply plodded through life, believing that I was in control of my own destiny.

Phantom made a full recovery, and I devoted myself to holding up my end of my bargain with God. I volunteered at the local animal shelter and did collections of food and blankets for the animals. I put my PR and event-planning skills to work in organizing events and fund-raisers for animal-related charities. The events I worked on were wildly successful—far exceeding the organization's goals—and every success felt like a sign from God and further fueled my craving for faith.

Just like everything else that I do in my life, I tackled this new march toward faith with laser focus. I enrolled in the Catholic Church's Rite of Christian Initiation of Adults (RCIA) program, bombarding the instructor with questions while everyone else just sat listening. I devoured every kind of book about the Christian faith that I could get my hands on, and I began reading daily the Bible my sister-in-law Sandy gave me when I began RCIA classes.

Then one day, faith became less of a project to be tackled and more of an intensely personal experience. I was alone in a quiet house and sitting on my bed, reading my new Bible, when I came to the section in the book of Matthew that includes the Sermon on the Mount. Included are these verses:

> For where your treasure is, there your heart will be also. . . . Therefore
> do not worry about tomorrow, for tomorrow will worry about itself.
> Each day has enough trouble of its own. (Matt. 6:21, 34)

Suddenly, it was like a bolt of lightning shot through me. The words jumped off the page. I felt this overwhelming surge of emotion, a swelling in my chest, and I began to cry. As I sobbed, I felt like the Holy Spirit was breathing new life into me. At that moment, I was changed forever.

I know now that God was placing His hand of protection over me to prepare me for three years of tragedies in my life. In January 2003, I lost my mother, and two other friends lost their mothers around the same time. Then another friend died after a battle with lung cancer, and, less than a year later, my friend Loree's husband committed suicide. She came to live with us for a time, where I waded through the trenches of grief with her day after day.

I believe now that, with those years of tragedies and a newfound faith burning inside me, God was preparing me for something big. Something that would test my willingness to step out in faith and take on a seemingly impossible challenge. I was primed for it, but I couldn't have anticipated what adventure God had intended for me.

Finally, God's challenge for me had arrived.

On the day I picked up that newspaper and looked into the eyes of Teeba, I could hear the words of my favorite Bible verse ringing in my ears: "Well done, good and faithful servant! You have been faithful with a few things; I will put you in charge of many things" (Matt. 25:23).

Those words are what I want to hear on the day I enter heaven.

So that day, as I stood there screaming at God on my driveway, I felt sure that helping Teeba was the impossible thing that He was calling me to make possible. I just knew this was the challenge that God had been preparing me for.

So why wasn't He helping me?

I'd kept my face tilted to the sky the entire time I was pleading with God, then I let my chin sink to my chest. That was when I saw it—a small golf marker lying on the ground by my foot. I picked it up and turned it over in the palm of my hand. On it were the words, "God Loves You," etched around a purple cross surrounded by laurel branches. I was sure it hadn't been there before.

The hair stood up on my arms, and all my anger and frustration dissolved into a feeling of calm. I began to cry. I'd been seeking some reassurance that I was doing the right thing, and feeling that I wasn't totally alone in my fears and frustration. I'd been screaming to God, and felt this was the sign that He was listening. It was a reminder that my time frame wasn't God's time frame. Whatever God wanted me to accomplish with Teeba, it would happen when the time was right.

I put that golf marker in a Lenox china case in the shape of a cross, where it remains today. A sense of peace came over me as I marched into the next phase of my journey knowing that God was on my side.

It wasn't long after that moment with the golf marker that we got our first big break.

I'd expressed my frustration about all the red tape to a friend who worked at a local television station, and she offered to connect me with Monica Robins, the station's health reporter, who is highly respected in our community. Monica agreed to the meeting, and on September 28, 2006, just more than two months after I'd read about Teeba, I showed up at the station clutching that newspaper article, now creased and dog-eared from all the times I'd trotted it around as I appealed to people for their help.

As I waited in the glass-enclosed lobby, I watched the buzz of activity in the newsroom as reporters dashed from their cubicles to the set and back. I had that same feeling of confidence and anxiety as I had when I met Dr. Fanaroff; I was determined to make Monica understand Teeba's plight and agree to help me.

"Barbara? Hi, I'm Monica Robins."

Tall, blond, and personable, Monica greeted me in the lobby and welcomed me into the conference room. She's known in town as being an honest, trustworthy reporter who asks the right questions and listens intently.

"How can I help you?" Monica asked, giving me her full attention.

I launched into my now well-practiced story about reading about Teeba and feeling compelled to do something to help her. By then, University Hospitals had already agreed to see Teeba, and now I just needed to figure out a way to get her here. My sense of urgency was building as was my frustration with the slow pace of progress.

She listened carefully through it all, then looked at me.

"I know just who to call—Steve Sosebee," she said. "He and his wife, Huda, founded the Palestine Children's Relief Fund. Let's call him right now."

Monica described Steve and Huda's work—they were located only an hour away from me, and their organization helps children from the Middle East get medical treatment in the West. At that time they'd brought more than seven hundred children to the United States, and Monica had recently done a story on their work.

Monica reached for the conference room speakerphone and dialed Steve's number. Miraculously, he was not only in the country but was sitting right by his phone to answer. After greetings and introductions, I again recounted Teeba's story and the work I had done so far to try to bring her here.

"Barbara," Steve interjected as soon as I stopped to take a breath. "I can help you."

Those were the words I'd been hoping to hear for so long—words that would put me on a path to move forward.

Teeba's case lined up well with the mission of the Palestine Children's Relief Fund (PCRF), but they'd never had a situation quite like mine—an American trying to help a specific child. Normally, they organize medical missions to go to the Middle East to provide treatment to children, or they take injured or sick children to other parts of the world for care. Typically, the PCRF acts as the sponsor of the injured child, bringing them here for specific treatment then returning them when the treatment is complete. This situation was different; Tim and I were acting as Teeba's sponsors.

Still, this was an amazing opportunity. They had the expertise to expedite the visas and funding to pay for transportation. They also had an apartment in Amman, Jordan, where they housed patients waiting to get the proper paperwork for trips to the United States. And they had a team of Arabic-speaking social workers who could make communication with Teeba's family easier, plus relationships within Northeast Ohio's Muslim community to provide support to them while they were here.

All of this was amazing news. It was clear that Steve knew his stuff, understood the culture, and could make my plan a reality.

Then he hit me with a reality check.

"The toughest part of this will be getting Teeba a visa to come to the United States," he said.

Steve confirmed some of what I'd already learned about the way our immigration system worked and the process for gaining entry into the United States. He explained the fundamentals—we would need to make sure Teeba had a passport, then she would have to apply to get a visa to enter the United States. And because there was no US Embassy in Baghdad at the time, she would need to go to Amman, Jordan, to apply.

I'd secretly been harboring grand plans to bring Teeba's entire family to Cleveland, but it became clear as Steve continued to talk that this would be impossible. One of the most important things the US government looks for when granting a visa is the person's intent to return to their home country. Bringing a whole family here from a poor, war-torn country would be out of the question.

"Your best chance of getting approved is to have Teeba come with one adult, and it has to be a female," Steve said. Considering that we were at war with Iraq, it would have been next to impossible for an Iraqi man to get a visa to enter the United States.

I shot rapid-fire questions at Steve, and he answered all of them patiently. After a thirty-minute conversation, I was overwhelmed by all of the information he had given me—everything I didn't understand and needed to. But there were only three words that were ringing in my ears as we ended the call: "I can help."

That was all I needed to hear.

Teeba's family was initially dismayed. We relayed the good news through Mahmood, the English-speaking relative who'd helped with our earlier communciations, that we'd found an organization willing to help—but also that Teeba would have to come with just one female adult. Both Dunia and Furat wanted to be here to provide support for Teeba during her treatments. Having Dunia come alone with Teeba would have been the logical choice, but there were some snags. Grandparents hold a great deal of decision-making power in Iraqi villages, and Teeba's paternal grandmother, Amal, would not permit Dunia to make the trip. Amal felt it would be inappropriate for a young woman to travel without her husband. Plus, Dunia had two young children at home, and while she and Furat were willing to leave two-year-old Fatima with her grandparents, she was still nursing four-month-old Aboody and couldn't leave him behind.

So, against Dunia's wishes, it was decided that Teeba would make the trip with Amal, a fifty-two-year-old woman who'd never been apart from her husband since they were married when she was sixteen years old.

Throughout that fall, I peppered Steve and Huda with constant emails asking for updates and requests to make the process go faster. Over and over, they explained there was nothing we could do on our end to speed things up.

My get-things-done personality had to settle in for a frustrating wait as we hit one roadblock after another. For example, Teeba had a passport but Amal did not. Long closures at the passport office in Baghdad delayed Amal from getting her proper documents until November, resulting in them missing their appointments at the Jordanian Embassy in Amman to apply for visas. After Teeba and Amal finally arrived in Jordan, the Iraqi government passed a law requiring new passports for all citizens—so they had to return to Iraq in January 2007 to have their passports reissued. With new passports in hand, they returned to Amman in March for another appointment. They made their visa applications, then settled in for a long wait with a host family while waiting for approval.

Through all of this, the violence in Iraq and Jordan continued to escalate, making each of these journeys dangerous for Teeba and her grandmother. I continued to push, contacting my legislators and others I thought might be able to help. Clearly, my priorities were not their priorities, and progress was slow. It was a frustrating time filled with constant ups and downs.

But I pushed on. I knew the moment would come when all the papers were signed and all the plans had been made—we just had to keep pushing.

"It's been almost a year and still nothing," I complained to my friend Carla Longano as we were on the golf course one day in late June 2007, hitting our approach shots to the eighteenth hole. I'd just passed the eleventh-month mark since I'd started trying to get Teeba here, and there was still no word when—or if—she might finally pass these last few hurdles and be able to come to the US.

It was a beautiful sunny day, and it felt good to be outside trying to focus on something else, rather than worrying constantly about Teeba. But she still always sat in the back of my mind, and I never went anywhere without my phone by my side with the ringer on, just in case I would get any news from the Sosebees. I restrained myself as best I could from pestering them constantly with questions and requests for updates.

Two other golfers were ahead of us, so Carla and I stood together near the green, talking and waiting for our turn. Then, from the other side of the fairway, I heard my phone ringing in our golf cart. I dropped the club I was holding and ran for the call. I got there just in time.

"Hello?" I said, a little out of breath from my mad dash back to the cart.

"Barbara? It's Huda," said my friend's familiar voice.

My chest clenched. She obviously had news—was it good news? Or bad news?

"So," she said, "when do you want her?"

I couldn't even answer. I burst into tears and fell to my knees right there on the fairway.

"She's coming! *Teeba's finally coming!*" I cried out to Carla, who rushed toward me and pulled me into a tight hug and broke down into tears herself. I couldn't believe that the moment I had dreamed about was finally going to happen.

Huda waited patiently on the other end of the line until I regained my composure, then the conversation got serious. We needed to pick a date, and it needed to be soon. Amal and Teeba had been waiting a long time, and we couldn't take any chances that another delay would arise while they were waiting.

The calendar was rolling around in my head. Independence Day was right around the corner, and I thought the sound of fireworks might be frightening to Teeba, coming from a place where explosions of a different kind were part of everyday life. We decided on a date a few weeks away: July 16, 2007. It was a while before the meaning of that date finally registered for me—that was exactly one year to the day since I first saw Teeba's penetrating dark eyes in our Sunday newspaper.

As I hung up the phone, I felt overwhelmed and overjoyed, but at the same time panicked. I'd wanted this for so long, but I still had no idea what to expect. The realization that this immense responsibility was actually coming to fruition was daunting. I knew I had to deliver. I couldn't disappoint Teeba, and I also couldn't disappoint all those who had gone the extra mile to help both of us. No more talk. It was time for action.

Carla and I quickly finished the eighteenth hole, jumped into the golf cart, and sped back to the clubhouse—her driving while I dialed Tim.

"Teeba's coming, Teeba's coming!" I shouted into the phone.

"Oh, honey, you did it!" he said. "You really did it!"

I raced home and into his arms, and I sobbed into his shoulder while he hugged me tight. As always, Tim was so solid and calming, even as the emotions of the past year burst out of me. He is, and always has been, my voice of reason and my rock.

Little did I know how much I would need Tim's calming presence as we faced the next steps in the process of helping this precious girl—steps that would become life changing for all of us involved. The past year had been a race; now we were embarking on a marathon. A whole new set of challenges was ready and waiting to smack us in the face.

I couldn't wait to begin preparing for Teeba's arrival. I tried to stay focused on my work, but my mind would often drift into dreaming about the big day. After work I would dash off to shop for the perfect gifts for Teeba and her grandmother. I picked out scented soaps for Amal, but I agonized over the right choices for Teeba. I wanted something that would be comforting and soft, something familiar I could give her when she got off the plane. I wanted something she could hold on to when she was afraid, coming to a new place thousands of miles from home—a place where she didn't speak the language and had no idea what was ahead of her.

About a week before she arrived, I popped into a Toys "R" Us store located just around the corner from a client's office. I paced the aisles looking for just the right gift, finally settling in front of a huge display of teddy bears in every color, shape, and design. I picked up each one and hugged it to my chest, envisioning how it would feel for Teeba to hold in her tiny hands, an image that brought tears to my eyes. I probably looked ridiculous, standing in a toy store in the middle of a summer day, hugging teddy bear after teddy bear for about an hour while tears flowed down my face.

Finally I found the perfect one that passed my hug test—a soft and sandy-colored bear with a big yellow bow with white polka dots. I headed to the checkout line, still crying and hugging this bear, prompting stares from the woman at the register and the other customers behind me in line. As I did often during those weeks, I had to restrain myself from bursting out to everyone around me with my amazing news: *Teeba's coming! Teeba's coming!*

CHAPTER 6

TEEBA: FROM SORROW TO HOPE

M y memories of those years after my accident come back to me through my senses. The smells, sounds, and sights of that time have pierced their way into my mind, preventing me from forgetting the little things. I remember the smell of the sand and the way my dad would bring the scents of the city into our house—what smelled to me like nickels and bonbon strawberry candies. I remember the feeling of my mom's warm embrace and the sounds of her crying.

After more than a month in the hospital, my sight began to come back. I was able to see perfectly, as the doctors had predicted, but it wasn't a blessing or a miracle to me. When my sight returned, I begged it to go away because I did not want to see the sadness and fear all around me. The people in my village were drowning in their tears while scary-looking men—who I later came to understand were Iraqi soldiers—stood every few feet, watching over our village.

Of course, worst of all, I saw my heartbroken parents trying so hard to carry on with their lives. I remember seeing them comfort each other. They would try to hide their crying faces from me, but I always knew what was wrong. I remember asking my mom constantly why she never smiled, and eventually both my parents would put weak smiles on their faces for my sake, even as they mourned Yousif's death and tried desperately to come up with ways to pay my medical bills.

My dad's devastation was visible in his face and his body. It was like everything he did took all the energy out of him. He would have just one conversation and then need to rest because he couldn't handle anything more for that day. Yousif was my dad's everything, his firstborn son—the son he planned to watch growing up for years to come. He sunk low, unable to budge or even think of moving a muscle at the news of his one and only son joining the angels, beyond his reach. My heart was heavy, too, even at such a young age. I can't help but conclude that the reason I felt such love for my brother for all the years I lived in Iraq is that God implanted empathy and compassion in my heart. I believe God wanted my heart to experience sadness to the lowest and joy to the highest, even as a toddler.

I remember visiting Yousif's grave a lot. It was an area set aside on flat, windy land, suffocated in dust. Families would come and lay rocks and pebbles on their loved ones' graves. I remember pocketing the most beautiful pebbles I found, the ones with intricate patterns or that shone in the sunlight, to take home with me. My mom would cry so hard she would lose her breath as we stood beside the grave. I can still hear her sobs and see the quiver of her lips as her heart broke.

But my memories of that time aren't all sorrowful. My mom often had trouble sleeping after Yousif's death, so we would all sit on the roof at night. She would stare and stare at the moon, and when my dad joined us he would hold me and tickle me. I recall my grandma, who owned the house and lived there with us, cooking like crazy—either to keep herself busy or to make sure her sons were eating during this time of mourning. My grandpa prayed more than ever before, waking up even before the sunrise prayer and praying twice as long. And when the rest of the family rose to start their days, he would stop each and every one of his sons and kiss them, whispering "*alḥamdulillāh*" ("all praises and thanks to Allah").

I don't remember my mother often calling me by my given name. She had little nicknames for me like *Tab-tab* (which sounds more like "tub-tub" in English) and *Tiubti* (pronounced like tie-OOB-tee). I remember the hammock I'd swing on in our front yard until I would nearly throw up. I remember munching on uncooked pasta with my cousins while we waited for dinner to be made. I remember staying up all night waiting to watch the cow's milk turn into yogurt, trying to prove my grandma wrong. There are other memories, too—ones I like to keep close to my heart, just for me.

The house where I grew up was in a village about sixty miles from Iraq's capital of Baghdad. My house was a handmade structure that stood two stories tall yet weak—gated on the perimeter, placed on the desert, the roof only covering half the house. We stayed in the covered part during the blazing hot days and in the uncovered part during the cooler evenings. The gate was rusty, but short enough that we could climb over it and hang by the stair railings. There was only one bedroom, with just one bed, but we lived with my grandpa and grandma, at least five of their sons (including my dad), their wives, and their children. My bed was the floor's embrace, a thin navy and red carpet with only a pillow. We all squeezed into that room, head to toe.

I loved visiting Baghdad. The city was beautiful—not a glittery or glossy kind of beauty, but the kind you can tell has been destroyed and rebuilt, making it that much more exquisite. Palm trees lined the roads, which—even if they were paved—were an obstacle course of potholes, rocks, and ditches. Sun burned on the ancient sand. The buildings that were still standing stretched up as high as twenty floors. Iraqi soldiers stood stoic, guns at the ready, around the borders of the city. There were times I remember gunshots ringing like a bell every hour and bombs shaking the ground every day. Those days might be followed by the silence of palm trees waving in the air, but the violence always returned.

Still, living in Iraq was not always devastating. There were those rare times when people might have seemed genuinely happy—if you didn't know about the violence all around them. Believe it or not, I remember music playing and people dancing in the streets when we visited Baghdad. Every time we had to go to the hospital, we would stop at a cafeteria next door for my favorite rice dish.

Although I loved going into the city, I hated taking the bus. It was dirty, rough, and crowded. But what I remember most were the stares. When their eyes landed on my face, all the people around me seemed to be holding their breath, as if I had some kind of contagious disease. The women's faces were full of judgment, and I could sense my mom tensing, trying to restrain herself from confronting them.

One day, we took the bus into the city for one of my doctor's appointments. I've always been observant, and as we were waiting for my name to be called, my eyes settled upon a teenage boy, accompanied by his father, who appeared to have water droplets forming on his fingers even though his hands were completely dry. It puzzled me, and I remember rubbing my little eyes to try to better see the boy's hands while we waited. My name was called, and we went into the doctor's office. Being the easily distracted kid that I was, I forgot all about the boy I'd been staring at.

About thirty minutes into our visit, I heard the first gunshots. A group of men charged into the doctor's office screaming and shooting. A man who worked at the hospital quickly guided my family and me into a bathroom, and told us to wait there until it was safe to come out. I cried and cried as my dad tried to hush me. We were silent as we waited. When we were finally able to come out of that room, I saw that teenage boy again. He was dead on the ground, still with the inexplicable droplets of water on his hands.

One very hot day, while my mother was home taking care of my baby brother, Aboody, my little sister Fatima and I got tired of running around the mosque, so we walked over to a lady selling purses in a nearby tent. It was there I saw a woman carrying explosives, with wires sticking out of the opening between her glove and her black sleeve. She was wearing a burka, a head covering that leaves only a woman's eyes exposed. I saw her put something that looked to me like bullets in one of the red purses while the saleswoman was talking to another client. Fatima and I ran home, and I never told my family what I saw. But that night, I could barely sleep, even in my mother's arms.

My grandfather had a farm behind our house, and I enjoyed playing with the animals there. One day I slipped out of my mother's arms while we were supposed to be napping and ran out to the farm. Two lambs had just been born and they were lying in the heat, making the most deafening shrieks. I decided they would be my new toys, so I filled up the baby pool we used to wash our clothes and used my baby brother's shampoo to give the lambs a bath. Little did I know the lambs were actually sick, almost dying in fact, and my grandpa had gone to get the vet. But by the time they returned, the cool bath had revived the overheated lambs. Everyone said I had cured them.

There was no one to cure me, though. I remember times when kids would stare at me and touch my scars, asking me if it hurt. They would pull off my hijab, or head scarf, exposing my scarred head; they would ask their parents right in front of me what was wrong with my face. People avoided me as if I were a leper. The hardest part was the parents who were clearly even more frightened of me than the children. It often made me cry, but sometimes I wouldn't even know it because my scarred skin could not feel the tears. When that happened, my mom always wiped my tears away— along with her own.

My face was always constricted. I could talk and hear normally, and cry lightly without pain. But if I cried hard like many kids do, my face would tighten and hurt me incredibly. I remember feeling like my scars hated me because not only could I not cry, scream, or get too angry, I also couldn't smile or laugh too hard. My face hurt the worst around my mouth, and I always felt pressure on my eyebrow area—something I still feel to this day.

It was hard to keep my hands clean with all the dust and lack of clean water in my village. With the scars and the dirt, warts grew on my hands. I remember eating pomegranates was my favorite thing, but the juice from the fruit would drip painfully down the sensitive skin and warts on my fingers and hands, and I would cry and rush to find clean water—somewhere, anywhere. Also, my ears sometimes played tricks on me. Even though my hearing wasn't damaged by the burns, the noise and vibration of bombs and gunshots created a loud ringing whenever things fell silent.

In public, I was considered ugly and hard to look at, but at home my parents made me believe I was a princess. Regardless of how disgusted people looked when talking about me, when I came home I truly believed I was pretty. My mom gave me a stick to use as a wand, which became my most special princess accessory. She and I would pretend to argue over which one of us was prettier, but we always agreed it was me in the end.

At night we would lay on the roof talking about what it meant to be pretty. My mom, above everyone, was the most beautiful and kind woman in my eyes. I always wanted to look like her, because looking like her included more than just a face. It meant compassion and strength.

That's what I wanted even more than smooth skin and new hair: strength.

While my house was always filled with excitement and children's laughter, no one had ever heard a scream as loud as mine when I heard that there was an American woman who wanted to bring me to the United States for medical treatment. As much as I wanted to rid myself of the pain of my scars, I hated the thought of leaving my family. I believed that they must hate me to send me away.

My parents were very protective. They never allowed us to watch the news, rarely let us step outside of our village, and scolded us for standing too close to a stove. For this reason, they had waited until the absolute last second to tell me about the plans for me to fly to America. I cried when I found out, but when I saw the picture of the American woman holding her fluffy white dog, I thought, *How bad can this really be?* I listened to the hushed conversations of my grandparents and parents as they debated who should take me to America, and finally my grandmother, whom I call Bibi, made the executive decision that she would be the one. I didn't know it at the time, but after I was burned Bibi refused to visit me in the hospital and didn't think my mother should either, since I couldn't see her anyway. Imagine my mom's surprise that this same woman would insist that she be the one to fly halfway across the world with me.

My last night in Iraq came just a few weeks later, and the reality of leaving my family began to sink in. I remember fish being served for dinner, but I refused to eat. I screamed in anger at my mom for sending me away. I thought she hated me, so I pretended to hate her too. I left without saying I loved her. I was selfish, but I know now that I was only a child who didn't know any better. I would do anything to take back my angry words from that last night—to tell her how amazingly strong she was for allowing me to leave.

Although I spent several months in Jordan with a host family before leaving for America, those months are a blur. My memories from that time come in flashes: Seeing a toothbrush for the first time. Eating Cheetos while riding a scooter. Praying what seemed like endless prayers before each meal, my mouth watering while I waited for them to be done. A package of toys and dresses arriving from my parents in Iraq, including a green toy Jeep that I still treasure to this day. My grandma teaching me how to write and pray in the correct way.

The last memory of Jordan is of Bibi waking me up early on the morning of our flight to the United States. I didn't realize it then, but I started the rest of my life that day.

CHAPTER 7

MEETING TEEBA

On July 16, 2007—one year to the day that I first read about Teeba in the newspaper—Tim and I waited at gate B3 at Cleveland Hopkins International Airport. We were there with a translator, as well as with Monica Robins, the TV reporter who'd connected me with the Sosebees, and her videographer. University Hospitals also had its director of media technology there, Don McClung, to document Teeba's arrival.

This was post-9/11, so we had to get special permission to gain access to the terminal. Our group got a special escort who took us through security and down the terminal to wait by the scheduled gate. While Don and the TV cameraman readied their equipment, I paced back and forth in front of the gate, clutching that soft teddy bear with the yellow and white polka-dotted ribbon and dreaming of the moment I would reach out to place it in Teeba's hands. Within minutes, I would meet in person the child who had captured my heart exactly a year ago. I had no idea what to expect when that flight arrived and Teeba walked into my life.

Finally, about 9:30 p.m., Teeba's scheduled flight, United 442, arrived. The camera-mounted lights flicked on and Don and the TV cameraman started rolling. Tim and I positioned ourselves a short distance from the cameras and bright lights, thinking it might be frightening to Teeba and Amal to come off the plane and immediately have cameras in their faces.

My anxiety and excitement peaking, Tim and I held hands and watched each passenger file off the jetway, searching for Teeba's face. As the pack of passengers dwindled down to a few stragglers, my heart sank. Then, finally, an airline agent came off the jetway, shaking his head.

"There's a good possibility that the Royal Jordanian flight was late," said the agent. "They missed the flight."

"Oh no, oh no," I murmured to Tim. "Oh, please don't tell me this."

Sure enough, Teeba and Amal had missed their connection in Chicago. They'd caught the next flight, but it wasn't scheduled to arrive until 11:42 p.m. Our group headed to one of the airport restaurants to get some food to pass the time, but I couldn't sit down, much less eat.

I spent those hours just pacing and praying, chewing on the inside of my cheek out of nerves. *God*, I prayed, *You can't have brought us this far for things to fall apart now.* I paced and watched the clock. The time seemed endless.

Then, it was time. We all staggered back into our same spots surrounding the gate. Don and the TV cameraman hoisted their heavy cameras back up onto their shoulders and switched on their lights. Tim came up beside me and grasped my hand tightly.

I looked into his face and he smiled down at me. I smiled back, so grateful for his love and support at that moment. "Oh, Tim, please let them be on this flight," I said. "They have to be on this flight." He gave my hand an extra squeeze, then we again took our places around the entrance of the jetway. My heart filled with anticipation. Once again, a procession of bleary-eyed passengers staggered off the plane, blinking and startled by seeing cameras recording them, not to mention the sight of me staring at them, struggling not to cry and clutching a teddy bear. Tim stood erect, stretching his neck to see every face, making him seem even taller than his six-foot-four-inch frame. Our eyes were glued to the gate.

The entire plane emptied. Then, finally, there was Teeba.

What struck me first was how tiny she was, even tinier than I'd expected—only thirty-two pounds even though she was five years old—standing barely to my waist. Clad in a pink shirt, skirt, and sandals, Teeba clung tightly to the hand of her grandmother, who wore a stern and bewildered expression and was clothed from head to toe in a black abaya and white hijab. She looked so out of place among the plane full of travelers from Chicago, many of them probably business commuters eager to get home after a long day. Clearly anxious to get off that plane, Amal was walking rapidly enough that tired little Teeba was half walking, half skipping to keep up.

Teeba looked terrified. She was confused and overwhelmed at being surrounded by a group of strangers with glaring lights and video cameras, strangers speaking a language she couldn't understand. She shyly shrunk against her grandmother while she rubbed her tired eyes, and Amal slipped off the floppy sunhat Teeba was wearing to show us her burned scalp and patchy hair.

I instinctually sunk to my knees to get to Teeba's eye level. As she haltingly walked toward me, all of the commotion going around us seemed to fade away. As I looked into Teeba's eyes—dark, frightened, and surrounded by thick ropes of scar tissue—I felt the same irresistible connection to her that I had when I first saw her picture in the newspaper. I felt as if I knew her after gazing into those eyes in photographs for so long, but to her I was just a stranger in a scary environment, sobbing and saying her name.

"Hi, sweetheart. Hi, Teeba," I said, my voice breaking. "My name is Barbara. This is for you. Would you like to have it?"

She warily accepted the bear while still clinging to her grandmother's leg, frightened, tired, and overwhelmed.

I stood for a moment to hug Amal, who was standing like a deer in the headlights as the translator chattered in Arabic, greeting her and trying to explain what would happen next. I returned to my knees in front of Teeba and tried to make that first connection with her in the best way I knew how. I placed my hand on my heart and said, "Barbara." Then I reached gently across to hers and said, "Teeba."

In that moment, all of the frustrations and struggles of the previous year, all of my worries and fears, all of the uncertainties of what this moment would mean for our lives—it all dissolved into the background. Teeba was here, the little girl who'd taken up residence in my heart a year ago. I knew instantly that no matter what happened next, Teeba would always have that spot in my heart.

I grabbed Amal's bag, and our little pack of commotion started to move toward baggage claim. The translator raced to keep up as Amal and I welcomed and thanked each other in languages neither of us could understand. Teeba clung to her grandmother's leg and cried, while Amal made a half-hearted attempt to comfort her. The translator explained to Amal and Teeba that they would be coming to our house that night because their room at the Ronald McDonald House would not be available for a few days.

"Is she hungry?" I asked the translator. I grabbed snacks. "Teeba, do you want some crackers?"

She just looked at me blankly, frightened and not understanding. I held out a cracker. Teeba looked at her grandmother, afraid to take it.

"Will you tell her how pretty she looks?" I appealed to the translator. "She is so beautiful."

Soon Don and the TV cameraman stopped rolling, the rest of our group dropped back a bit, and with a little space I saw Teeba finally begin to relax. She smiled for the first time, and she began opening up in her tiny five-year-old voice to the translator.

"She says that Barbara is her friend," the translator told me. "She is forgetting all about the hard things of the trip because she is finally here."

Now nearly 1:00 a.m., we moved quickly through the terminal and baggage claim to get them home, so they could go to sleep. Our group slowly disbanded as we said our goodbyes to Monica, Don, and the translator. Tim came around with the van, and we loaded up Amal's and Teeba's bags safely in the trunk and all climbed into our seats.

When the doors shut, the van plunged into what seemed like deafening silence after coming from the chaos of the airport. Reality hit us hard—we were sitting in a car with two strangers from a rural village on the other side of the world who spoke no English and had zero exposure to American culture.

Tim and I just looked at each other, wordlessly communicating our bewilderment and exhaustion.

"Okay, we're off!" I said, brightening, trying to fill up the silence. "Are you hungry? I packed some turkey sandwiches. Or vegetables? Water?"

Of course, they couldn't understand what I was saying, but they both silently shook their heads at the food I was offering them. That night and for the next several days, they were afraid to eat food we offered, not knowing whether it might contain pork or other ingredients that they, as Muslims, were not permitted to eat.

The thirty-minute drive home from the airport seemed endless.

Amal sat stiffly, with her hands folded on her lap. Teeba wavered between total exhaustion and falling asleep on her grandmother's shoulder, to then perking up and curiously, but cautiously, looking around at everything out the window.

"So, when we get home . . ." I started to say, without thinking, glancing into the back seat. I'd momentarily forgotten that they couldn't understand me, but their blank faces staring back at me were certainly a reminder. Awkwardly, I smiled and reached back to pat Amal's arm and squeeze her hand, to no reaction.

"Are they okay?" Tim asked me. "Do you think they want some water?"

I laughed helplessly. "Honey, how am I supposed to know?"

I couldn't help thinking that if the situation were reversed, I would be terrified of being driven by strangers to an unfamiliar house in a foreign country, with no ability to communicate. What did they think of us? We just tried to slow everything down—making careful movements, speaking in a low tone of voice, and keeping a gentle demeanor. We didn't want to do anything that might frighten them.

But as soon as we arrived home and walked through our door, the silence erupted into chaos as Phantom came to the door barking at these new and unfamiliar guests. Amal jumped back and Teeba nearly leapt into her grandmother's arms as they both screamed in fear. Even though Phantom was a sweet and innocent little puff of white fur and was as harmless as dogs come, he was terrifying to them. In Iraq, dogs are not really a part of the family as they are in the United States. I later learned that Amal had once been bitten hard by a dog on her upper thigh.

We got them calmed down and ushered them inside. They were wide-eyed as they entered, taking in their first sights of an American home so different from their own—a suburban colonial with three bedrooms and two-and-a-half bathrooms, big enough for everyone to have their own rooms. Here, Teeba and Amal each had their own king-sized bed with a pile of pillows.

Teeba still clung tightly to her teddy bear, but as we entered her room, I presented her with another special gift. That year, Tickle Me Elmo was a huge sensation, and people were in a buying frenzy to get their hands on one. The hype for this little red Elmo who bent over laughing then fell to the floor was causing a mad rush at the local toy stores. My friend Maria—like me, determined and unwilling to accept the word *no*—set out to get one for Teeba, even as people were lining up to get them and even paying a premium to resellers when they sold out. But Maria, who'd met with the manager of a local Toys "R" Us armed with the article about Teeba, had managed to get a Tickle Me Elmo donated. She even had to have it wrapped in plain paper before she left so no one could see that she had one. That's just how Maria is—always there for me and ever resourceful.

I set it on the ground, and Teeba stared at the bright red furry creature, arms outstretched and black mouth open wide, in confusion. Then, gently, I tickled Elmo's stomach and watched her face for a reaction. Despite her exhaustion, Teeba burst out laughing at the doll's antics, turning it on and off over and over. Exhausted and confused, Amal just stared at the strange battery-powered creature.

As tired as they were, I had to make sure they understood how to use the plumbing in the bathroom. I turned on the left faucet and let it get a little steamy.

"This is the hot water, see?" I said, unable to stop myself from explaining things out loud even though I knew they couldn't understand me. I pantomimed sticking my finger into the hot water, pulling back quickly, saying "ouch," and blowing on my finger.

"And this is the cold," I said, turning on the right faucet, touching the cold water and performing an elaborate shiver, hugging myself and rubbing my upper arms. Amal clearly got the point, and explained it to Teeba in Arabic.

It would take several days before they realized that toilet tissue should be flushed away, as opposed to being left on the floor or in the wastepaper basket. It started a daily game of charades, trying to communicate with one another when no translator was there. It was a question of safety—I had to make sure they knew how to identify shampoo, cleaning supplies, or aspirin. Eventually we had Huda write down directions in Arabic to help them.

As Teeba and Amal prepared for bed, I left for a few moments. I wanted to stay with Teeba, scoop her up, and hold her in my lap, but I was able to discern that a display of affection like that from a stranger would not be received comfortably. Tim and I are huggers, but it was easy to read in Amal's body language that she and Teeba were more conservative. I'd been waiting to meet her for a full year, so it took everything I had to resist my body's urge to march into her room and smother this adorable little girl in hugs and kisses.

Go slow, I told myself. *Be patient. Give them space.*

Summoning every ounce of restraint, I hugged them each lightly goodnight. As I came downstairs to go to our room, I kept thinking how much I wanted to go back up and hug them again. But I didn't.

Tim and I didn't sleep well that night.

"It's hard to believe this is really happening," Tim said to me as we lay awake, staring at the ceiling where, just above us, the little girl I had become so attached to from afar was sleeping. "Quite honestly, Barbara, I knew you could get her here, but the chances of it not happening were pretty much equal."

I was just as incredulous. In my gut I'd always known it would happen, but it was still surreal. As scary as it was, we were ready to do whatever God called us to do to help her and her family.

I was ready, keeping the message of that golf marker fixed in my mind. *God loves you.*

CHAPTER 8

TEEBA: COMING
TO AMERICA

When my grandma and I stepped off what felt like a massive plane into Cleveland, Ohio, two things were going on in my mind: First, I was so grateful to exit the plane—mainly because it was freezing! I was only wearing a short-sleeved dress and sandals, and my body was so unfamiliar with the lack of warmth that I ended up throwing up on the first plane. I had never experienced a temperature so cold that it caused me to grit my teeth. I was shivering the entire time, and the blankets were as thin as the ones I remember nurses handing out in the hospital, so they were no help in providing any comfort.

Second, I was ravenously hungry. Even though I hated cheese, I remembered Bibi stuffing a few million packages of Laughing Cow cheese into her suitcase for the trip, and I was hoping she would offer to take a few pieces out for me. She never did, so my stomach continued to growl. I was five years old and only thirty-two pounds, and though I wasn't accustomed to colossal and lavish meals, I obviously still needed food. Apparently my grandma had forgotten about that, so I hadn't eaten for the ten hours prior to landing in Cleveland. My grandma was suspicious of the food in America and wouldn't let me eat on the plane or in the airport.

By the time our plane approached the Cleveland airport, all I wanted was to sleep in a warm, comfortable room, eased of my fears, with a belly full of cow cheese.

When we landed, Bibi grabbed my arm and started dragging my body alongside her, disregarding my complaints and whining. I was too exhausted to stand up straight, but I knew better than to disobey Bibi. We walked out the long tunnel connecting the airport to the plane. When we stepped into the terminal, Barbara, Tim, reporters, and a translator stood eagerly waiting to meet us. All the people, cameras, and lights would have been a little startling to most kids in that situation, but I was so tired I barely noticed.

I remembered seeing the photograph of Barbara and her little white dog while I was still in Iraq, so I felt relieved to find her familiar face. My first thought was, *Wow, her hair is very light.* That's a strange thing to find fascinating, but I had never seen blond hair before. Even crazier to me was the fact that both Tim and Barbara had light blue eyes that did not blend into their pupils like those of my family and me. It was a shocking sight to five-year-old me.

That's when Barbara reached out her hand to give me a gift that would grab the attention of any child—a fluffy, heavenly stuffed bear with a vibrant yellow bow. I later named her Binti Shatra, meaning "good girl." I still love my Binti Shatra today.

The stuffed bear was comforting, but all I could really think of was finding food and warmth. I heard Barbara speaking to me, but even if I had understood English back then, her words wouldn't have registered with me. I was so exhausted that I'd started to tune out all the chaos swirling around me—until Bibi threatened a scolding. Then I straightened myself up and tried to appear as though I slightly understood what was happening.

Many people kept taking my little hat off my head, which Bibi had prepared me for. Even though I was always ashamed of my exposed head, I tried to stay graceful because I remembered Bibi telling me that people would want to see my face and my head. She told me people would stare at me, but instead of ridiculing me, they would be staring so they could attempt to fix the damage the explosion had done to my face and scalp. As the young, pretty translator talked to my grandma about how long the Marlowes had been waiting for us, I was wondering how long we would have to wait to get to their house.

Bibi wouldn't let me eat any of the food Barbara and Tim brought because we couldn't be sure what was in it. But the translator was Muslim, so Bibi let me eat the crackers she gave me. I devoured them, and before I knew it, we were at the Marlowes' house. As I stepped inside, I thought I'd just entered a palace. The floors glistened with green and black marble, the fridge was stocked with all kinds of food, and the beds were topped by actual mattresses—not just a sheet lying on the floor. They were the kinds of beds I had only ever seen on television at home.

It was nearly 1:30 a.m., and just as Bibi was ready to drop from exhaustion, I was getting my second wind. I climbed up on the king-sized bed Barbara had offered to us and jumped on the mattress like it was a trampoline. Bibi yelled at me continually to stop, afraid the floor would collapse. I jumped higher, imagining the bed breaking under my weight, just like the stacks of pillows would crumble as my cousins and I leapt onto them back in Iraq. Finally Bibi picked me up and physically placed me on the bed, instructing me to change out of my clothes and go to sleep. This time I obeyed.

I woke up to the soothing feeling of Barbara scratching my back with her long nails, as my eyes drooped once again. Barbara was so gentle and kind to me. It was obvious that all she wanted was to help me. She examined my hands, which were dark, scarred, swollen, and covered with warts. Barbara made it her mission to get rid of the warts, just the first of many ways she was always working to bring me to good health.

Barbara shared some of the same traits as my mom—caring, always knowing how to make me laugh, and always saying no to things before giving in and letting me have my way. All of this made it easier to feel at home, even in such a strange place.

Even from those earliest days, Barbara helped fill the void of missing my mom.

CHAPTER 9

WARM WELCOME

The next morning ushered in a gorgeous July day, warm and sunny with a gentle breeze. I remember feeling how lucky we were to have such a perfect day for Teeba, a day when she could be outside and safe. No bombings or explosions, nothing to fear—except of course Phantom, although at sixteen years old, he had no desire to be around a little girl and completely ignored her.

Once Teeba and Amal got up, Teeba's mood was completely changed from the night before. She was curious and fascinated by every new thing she came across. The flush of the toilet was frightening, but the refrigerator was a wonder to her, containing endless amounts of food and especially cold bottled water. "*Ma'an!*" she exclaimed every time she wanted a bottle of water.

Amal was reserved, still hesitant to eat for fear that alcohol or pork would cross her lips. I finally convinced them to eat a banana and drink some tea and water, but that was it.

When I'd unpacked their suitcases the night before, I found that they'd prepared themselves for the likelihood that their dietary options would be limited—they'd packed what seemed like pounds of little white circular packages of Laughing Cow cheese and mango juice boxes. Everything was crushed and warm, but I salvaged what I could and put it in the refrigerator.

We'd invited all of our friends and family over for a party that day to celebrate Teeba's arrival, so I spent the morning bustling around the house, cooking and getting ready. Tim grabbed Phantom's leash to take him for a walk, and Teeba—wary of strangers and especially men—shocked all of us by stepping forward to go with him. I stopped cutting vegetables to watch this moment. Gently he extended his hand, she slipped her tiny hand in his, and they headed out the door, her head barely reaching his waist. He glanced back my way with a meaningful look and a smile growing on his lips.

Later he told me how emotional that first physical connection between them was. How astounded he was by the fact that on this otherwise normal day, he was out taking a walk with a little burned five-year-old girl from Iraq who spoke no English. While I'd become obsessed with helping Teeba from the first moment I saw her in the newspaper, Tim reached that turning point when he saw her walk off that plane. In that moment, less than twenty-four hours after she'd arrived, Teeba gave Tim her trust and her heart, and he gave his to her in return.

Carla and her son Nick, who was the same age as Teeba, were among the first to arrive. Carla had explained to Nick in advance what had happened to Teeba and why she looked different, but with the openness of a child, he never reacted to her appearance or asked any questions. He handed her a bouquet of hydrangeas left over from his aunt's wedding the previous day. Then Carla gave Teeba her first gift—a pink Disney princess dress with a crown. The Disney princesses were popular in Iraq as well, and Teeba immediately dashed upstairs to pull the dress over her clothes. Moments later, she paraded down the stairs like a true princess in the dress with the crown on her little bald head—upside down. She looked so happy I didn't try to fix it before she ran off with Nick to play with the coloring books and soccer ball he'd brought with him.

Throughout the day, about thirty friends and family members flowed in and out of our house. Steve and Huda came and thankfully brought Arabic food like pita bread, hummus, and tabbouleh that was familiar to Teeba and Amal.

Every guest brought Teeba a gift—toys, clothes, stuffed animals. She pulled open each package with a look of wonder, eyes wide, hunting through the boxes to uncover the toy inside. She put on every piece of play jewelry she received, and soon she was dripping in plastic bling. At first she seemed to be guarding her toys, afraid to leave them unsupervised. But then, one present came in a particularly large Dora the Explorer gift bag, and she made that the repository for all of her gifts. She dragged that bag behind her throughout the house, placing each new gift carefully inside, seemingly afraid that someone would take the gifts if she didn't keep them with her.

"Huda, could you please tell Teeba that all those toys are hers to keep forever and that no one will take them away from her?" I asked Huda. She'd previously told me that Teeba didn't have very many toys at home in Iraq, and the ones she did have had to be shared with her two younger siblings.

As Huda translated, a grin of excitement and relief spread over Teeba's face. One particularly thick rope of scar tissue pulled down the right side of her lip at that time, so every smile was adorably crooked.

"*Shukraan*," she replied. Thank you.

"*Afwan*," I responded. You're welcome.

Monica was there with her videographer, interviewing Steve, Huda, Amal, Tim, and me about this whirlwind experience for a news report that would air in a few days. My effort to keep media attention on Teeba's plight was limited and strategic—I knew that getting her story out there was the way I could uncover people willing to help her. It was also a good opportunity to get the word out there about the work that Steve and Huda were doing through the PCRF.

"That this complete stranger went through the effort of bringing this child here just by reading her name in the newspaper completely offsets and undermines everything Al-Qaeda and the terrorists are trying to say about us," Steve told Monica. "Maybe they'll be able to change the way some people think about Americans when they go home."

For a child who had been in the United States less than twenty-four hours, spoke no English, and was thousands of miles away from her mother's arms, Teeba made herself completely at home. Even though she was in an unfamiliar place surrounded by strangers, she went fearlessly throughout the house yelling "*shileeny!*" ("pick me up"). She climbed up on Carla's shoulders, chased Nick around the yard, and reveled in the attention of our guests.

I watched her in wonder. *She's here. She's really here.*

On that day, Amal talked comfortably with Huda, but when Huda was not around, Amal's discomfort was evident in her body language. Throughout the commotion, hugs, and laughter of the party, Amal could usually be found sitting alone in a patio chair, separated from the rest of our guests. I wanted to make her feel included, like part of our family, but had no idea how to bridge that distance between us.

Amal was stern and stoic, the exact opposite of my demonstrative, affectionate way. As Monica interviewed her on camera, she politely told Huda how honored she was to meet us and how Teeba could not have been here without us. Hearing that, I reached over to lightly squeeze her hand, but she didn't respond. She just continued to sit stiffly erect.

She smiled only rarely, and her face and hands—the only parts of her body she ever exposed—looked older than her fifty-two years. She never wore makeup or painted her nails. In most of the pictures we have of her, she is standing still with her arms rigid at her side while someone attempts to put their arm around her.

And yet that very first day is when I have my memory of her at her happiest. After our guests had left, we all drove to Carla's house, since she had a swing set that Teeba and Nick could play on. While the kids were running around the yard and slurping popsicles, Amal wandered over to the swing, sat down, and pushed off. Swinging back and forth, her black abaya fluttering around her, a huge smile appeared on her face and she even laughed. It was the first and only time I saw her appear to be enjoying herself.

Toward Teeba, Amal was definitely not the kind of warm-and-fuzzy grandmother that Americans think of. She was a strict disciplinarian, rarely demonstrating love, affection, or empathy, even when Teeba was frightened by her unfamiliar surroundings. When she gave Teeba a bath, she scrubbed her sensitive skin so hard that Teeba would cry out in pain.

Communication with Amal was difficult, but her disapproval of the American dress and lifestyle was evident in her body language and expressions. Underneath that hard exterior, though, I knew she was also terrified. She was the matriarch of the family and was accustomed to being in control. Here, she had lost all control of her surroundings. I tried to keep in mind how she must have been feeling instead of judging her strict tone and behavior.

With the trusting heart of a child, Teeba warmed up to us immediately. She soaked in the love and genuine concern of all those around her. Each day she became more confident, more friendly, and visibly reassured that we loved her and wouldn't hurt her. At every shout of "*shileeny!*" we gathered her up in our arms. She would wrap those tiny little burned hands around our necks and nestle her face close, all thirty-two pounds of her sitting on our shoulders or hips. Every time those big, dark soulful eyes looked into mine, my heart swelled more and more with affection for this child.

Moving day.

We just about needed a moving crew to take Teeba's new toys to their room at the Ronald McDonald House when it became available a few days later, though some stayed at our house. There are Ronald McDonald Houses around the country, and they serve as temporary homes to families who have to travel to faraway places for medical treatment. The exterior of the house is warm and welcoming, not at all institutional. Inside, it's big enough for fifty-five families to stay there, with family lounges, a kids' playroom, and outdoor playgrounds and gardens. The kitchens are enormous, with giant refrigerators where residents can store their own food and enough space for them to prepare their own meals too. Volunteers also come in to cook meals for everyone, but Amal never permitted Teeba to eat food prepared by others.

As we headed into the house on that first day, our arms filled with Teeba's new treasures, Amal and Teeba slowly looked around at their new temporary home but had no reaction. Teeba saw other little kids running around, and I could tell she wanted to run off with them but wouldn't dare without Amal's approval.

I knew it would be good for them to have a few other Arabic speakers around. There was even one Muslim family there at the same time, with a little girl just a bit older than Teeba, although Amal kept her granddaughter on a tight leash around the other children. But even though I knew that being there was best for them, Tim and I were a mixed bag of emotions as we left that day. My heart broke at the idea of being separated from Teeba, whom I'd become very attached to, very quickly.

So I did everything I could to be sure I saw Teeba as much as possible. I threw myself into the role of activities director. We started with a trip to the zoo with my brother-in-law George and my sister-in-law Sandy, where Teeba played on the playground with other children and marveled at animals from all over the world. Everywhere we went, people stared at Amal because of her dress—a devout Muslim, she wore a hijab and an abaya every day—and she was clearly shocked by the way American women dressed in the summer. The only time she uncovered her head was when we were at home alone without Tim there.

Feeling adventurous, I once took them to a skateboarding tournament near the shore of Lake Erie, having no idea what to expect. I thought Teeba might enjoy seeing kids doing acrobatics on skateboards. But it was clearly the wrong choice for Amal, who was horrified by the sight of girls wearing skin-tight T-shirts and shorts as short as they could get, plus spiked green hair, tattoos, and piercings. Teeba just seemed amused. While we were there, I jumped behind a sign, motioned to her, and put my finger to my lips. She immediately picked up on what I was up to and quietly ran to join me. When Amal and Tim came along, we jumped out and frightened them. Teeba and I both cracked up into laughter.

We cut that outing short and headed instead to the Cleveland Botanical Gardens, where Amal walked through the lush foliage and Teeba played in the dancing fountains, then we picked up ice cream before dropping them back off at the Ronald McDonald House. Every goodbye was excruciating. My heart would ache every time I had to drive away and leave Teeba there.

By now Amal and I had begun calling each other *okht*, the Arabic word for "sister." In her tiny, sweet voice, Teeba called us Mama Barbara and Papa Tim.

CHAPTER 10

TEEBA: GOLDEN LOCKS

My first memory of my first day in America was the bouquet of flowers I received from Nick, who would become my very first friend here. Barbara and Carla, Nick's mom, were some of the most beautiful women I had ever seen. They both had golden blond hair, eyes shiny blue and gorgeous green respectively, and they were so motherly toward me. I recall waiting in the driveway, playing with a ball, before being called into the house to get dressed in the princess gown Carla brought for me. I felt like a true princess as I paraded down the staircase of Barbara's home dressed in the princess gown, tiara upside down on my head, and carrying Nick's bouquet.

Barbara and Tim's friends and family showered me with gifts of stuffed animals, clothes, chalk, and just about everything else you could think of. I remember opening presents, blowing bubbles, and running in the grass, but I can't recall too much else of the day. Except that there was a little girl, Huda's daughter Jenna, who reminded me of my sister Fatima. Playing with this little girl made me remember how much I missed home.

My memories of home came back to me as I noticed what soft hair she had, just like Fatima. My mom used to sit Fatima on a ledge by the gate of our house to braid her hair, and I would sit on the ground and watch. Then as soon as my mom would go into the house, I would take my sister's braids out so I could play with her hair. Looking at Jenna, I thought about how much I missed that. But after less than twenty-four hours in America, I already felt happy and safe in the Marlowes' house.

After a few days, Bibi and I moved all our things into the Ronald McDonald House. I don't remember much about living there, except that Bibi restricted me from doing a lot of the things I was tempted to do. Like talk to non-Muslim families or eat a hamburger. There was a little girl there at the same time who was also Muslim, and she would sneak hamburgers out of the dining area and try to tempt me to eat them with her.

But I know Bibi loved me. I love Bibi, too, I really do. She made me the best Arabic food, and she made sure I was okay at all times—not okay as in happy, but just not bleeding or dying or anything like that. But she is a traditional Arab grandmother who did not always show the kind of grandmotherly love that Americans are familiar with. Arab grandmothers, and often mothers, too, have a stereotype of being extremely strict and never smiling.

Like when I finally got my first wig—I never really knew if Bibi liked it or not. Bibi was not the type of person to praise someone's good looks or even point them out. I decided I wanted to get a blond wig, because Barbara and Carla were so pretty with blond hair. That was the hair color I thought everyone in America had to have. But I didn't care if Bibi liked it or not. I did, and that was all that mattered.

One of my few clear memories of our time at the Ronald McDonald House was a call we got from my dad while Bibi and I sat in our room. He was calling with bad news—his sister, Bibi's daughter, gave birth to a son who died in his sleep a few hours after. Bibi was devastated. But simply hearing my dad's voice made me upset as well. On days like these, Bibi and I both missed home.

She was the only person in America who felt the way I did—grateful but sad.

REALITY CHECK

Swiveling her head to gape at all of the sample wigs surrounding her, Teeba climbed up into Jeffrey Paul's salon chair. Her eyes were wide and her crooked smile was growing on her face as she realized that this was the moment she'd dreamed of. She was finally getting a wig.

"Who's this pretty lady?" Jeffrey cooed to Teeba. He gently slipped off the new Cleveland Indians hat that she'd just received as a gift, revealing her scarred scalp. The hair she did have was pulled back into a low ponytail.

More than half of Teeba's scalp was burned in the explosion. Other than a small wisp just above her forehead and thin hair over her ears, her hairline starts just behind the crown of her head. She always wore the hair she did have long, but it couldn't hide the additional burned patches at the back of her head. Because third-degree burns damage the inner and outer layers of skin, her hair follicles were destroyed and can never grow hair again in those areas of her scalp.

Our entourage of Teeba, Amal, Maria, Huda, and me clustered around Teeba in a private room at Jeffrey's salon, along with Jeffrey's wife, Zina, Wigs for Kids executive director Susan Ross, and Monica Robins and her videographer. The room was designed for customers to have a comfortable, private place to try on wigs.

Jeffrey had started Wigs for Kids back in 1981 after his fifteen-year-old niece lost her hair during chemotherapy. The organization collects donations of real hair from all over the world to make custom wigs for kids who lose their hair due to cancer, alopecia, burns, or other medical conditions. The wigs are free to these children, but each one would normally cost several hundred dollars and have to be replaced frequently as a child grows. It also has to be durable with extra adhesives so the child can still play on the playground, participate in sports, and even go swimming without worrying that the wig might come off.

In this room there was a display of sample wigs sitting atop mannequin heads, and hair samples in every color you can imagine. Teeba was beaming like a kid in a candy store. She said something quietly to Huda.

"She says she wants to be blond," Huda announced, and we all laughed—Teeba had the dark hair and olive skin of a typical Iraqi, so blond didn't seem like the right fit. But she was insistent.

"All of the Arabic girls like Teeba want to be blond because of Barbie," Huda told us. And, I would learn later, she wanted to be blond like me too.

Jeffrey plucked off the shelf a sample wig in a good compromise shade—a dark blond that gave her what she wanted while still coordinating with her skin tone. As he placed the long hairpiece over her head, it momentarily covered her face. Teeba reached up with her tiny hands and parted the hair around her face, pulling it back like curtains on a stage. Looking in the mirror, her face was one of pure joy. She was seeing herself with hair for the very first time in her memory.

"*Hilwah!*" I said, calling her beautiful, as everyone else complimented her too.

Teeba was a little dismayed when he took the dark blond wig off to take careful measurements of her head, but she sat still and patient, clearly dreaming of taking that wig home with her. But it wouldn't be today. Her smile faded into disappointment as Huda told her that it would take about a month for her wig to be crafted. For now, she'd be going home empty-handed.

It was hard to know what kind of medical treatment Teeba's parents thought she'd receive when they sent her off to the United States with her grandmother. They probably had about the same expectations as Tim and I—a few surgeries, a new wig, and some medications they couldn't access in Iraq, then she'd be flying back home within a few months. From our earliest visit with Dr. Fanaroff, the hospital staff had cautioned us that they couldn't come up with a treatment plan or any kind of timeline for Teeba until they evaluated her.

It was during that evaluation that a big, fat reality check smacked us right between the eyes.

A week after Teeba arrived, we sat in the office of Dr. Arun Gosain, head of craniofacial pediatric plastic surgery at Rainbow Babies & Children's Hospital. It was as if he had arrived in Cleveland as a special gift from God just for Teeba—transferring from a hospital in Wisconsin to take this job at Rainbow just a few weeks before Teeba's first appointment, and with nationally known expertise. He had the perfect demeanor for caring for a young, scared child. He was slight in stature with a gentle bedside manner. His soft-yet-straightforward voice put everyone in the room at ease, and he spoke directly to Teeba at eye level.

We were all packed into Dr. Gosain's evaluation room—Teeba, Amal, Huda, my friend Paula Holm, Don McClung, and I. Dr. Gosain's nurse, Randi, was there, along with the hospital's medical photographer, Apryll, who took photos of Teeba's scars. We watched as Dr. Gosain explored every inch of Teeba's burned face, scalp, and hands. She was timid and shy but never objected to his examination.

Dr. Gosain began to explain the options for treatment of Teeba's scars while Huda translated. The first option was a procedure known as split-thickness skin grafting. It would involve harvesting the upper layers of skin from another part of her body—usually the legs, abdomen, or another part of the body that can be covered with clothing—and grafting it over the injured skin. Her doctors in Iraq had attempted a split-thickness graft soon after her injury, using skin from her thigh, but it didn't make a significant improvement in replacing her scars. This would be the least invasive option, but wouldn't produce the kind of results her family and we were hoping for, so Dr. Gosain advised against it.

The second option involved local tissue rearrangement and skin grafts, which would help with the uncomfortable tightness in Teeba's skin and obstruction to her nasal passages, and could be done in a single stage so that she could return home more quickly. The downside was that it would do nothing to improve the aesthetics of Teeba's burn injuries; it would only ease her discomfort.

Dr. Gosain recommended a third option—an extensive process of reconstruction called tissue expansion, in which he was a nationally known expert. Tissue expansion relies on the body's own ability to grow new, healthy skin. Dr. Gosain would insert a balloon-like device under the uninjured skin, and each week he would gradually fill the balloon with saline, gently stretching it to be used in a surgical graft a few months later. It would be a full-thickness graft, meaning he would harvest all layers of skin and use it to replace the damaged skin, giving Teeba her best shot at aesthetic improvement.

To get an evenly matched skin tone, the expander would have to be placed as close to her face as possible, starting with one just under her right jawline. Once the expander was big enough to produce the right amount of skin for the injured area—about the size of a large potato—it would be taken out, the burned skin on her right cheek would be removed, and the new skin would be stretched upward and attached to her face. To generate skin for her forehead, he would place a second expander on her upper back.

I gazed at Teeba's face. Even if she had understood English, she wouldn't have had a clue what we were talking about. I allowed myself for a moment to imagine her face with clear, smooth skin. But it was hard not to think about the trauma it would take for her to get there. In the shocking pictures that Dr. Gosain showed us of tissue expanders in other patients, the expanders made them look like they had enormous tumors. I couldn't imagine Teeba having to walk around with these things bulging out of her neck and back, and the stares she would get, probably far worse than the stares that her burns created. He hadn't even gotten to the point of addressing whether he could do anything about her scalp and ears.

"This would be done over multiple stages of expansion and grafting," Dr. Gosain explained, "which will require several surgeries." After the first skin graft was complete, he added, more rounds of tissue expansion would be needed to generate skin for her left cheek and nose.

"Plus, reconstructive surgery is unpredictable," Dr. Gosain said. "It's difficult to speculate how many surgeries and how much time will be required to give Teeba the treatment she needs. But my initial assessment is that she will need to be here at least two years."

I was stunned into silence.

I felt increasingly overwhelmed by my feelings for Teeba. I was getting very attached to her, and I'd already entertained secret fantasies of her being able to stay here forever. But those were just daydreams. Now, here was Dr. Gosain saying that if she was going to get the help she needed, she would *have* to stay here, not months but years. That little private daydream now collided with reality, and a million questions started running through my head: Now what do we do? Will her family want her to stay or come home? What is our responsibility to this child now? Can we commit to this? Will it be the right thing for her?

But then a sense of peace washed over me. I had willfully and eagerly accepted the path that God laid before me. If He had confidence in me, I had to have confidence in Him that He would make everything turn out for the good. I needed to believe He loved me, trusted me, and would guide me. From that, I derived peace.

There was never any doubt in my mind that we would see this through, no matter how long it took. I resolved to look at each step in short increments of time. It was just too daunting when I looked far down the road and permitted all of those racing questions to penetrate my brain. But in one regard there was no question—we were all in. Teeba looked at me with so much trust in her eyes, I couldn't let her down.

Then I turned to watch Amal as Huda relayed the news about how long Teeba's treatment would take. She didn't say a word, but I could see the shock and anxiety spread across her face as the news sunk in that Teeba wasn't going to just get a surgery and some creams and head home. Not only had Amal never been separated from her husband before but Huda also told us that Amal was terrified that he would take another wife in her absence.

Of course, Teeba didn't understand anything about what this news could mean for her and her family. She only had one question.

"Can you make my face beautiful?" she murmured in her sweet voice, translated by Huda.

"It's going to take a long time and many surgeries, but yes, we're going to make you even more beautiful than you already are," he responded, as she grinned shyly.

I wanted nothing more for her. But if that was going to happen, Teeba wouldn't be returning home to her parents in Iraq any time soon.

CHAPTER 12

A LIFE OF STRUGGLE

Furat and Dunia are a modern-day version of Romeo and Juliet—star-crossed lovers drawn to each other despite their families' and communities' disapproval. He is Shia and she is Sunni, two sects of the Muslim faith that have been deeply divided for more than a thousand years.

Marriages between religious sects in the rural regions of Iraq where they live are unusual, but not unheard of. Still, Dunia's and Furat's families were staunchly opposed to their relationship right from the start. The couple met while walking to school, when Dunia was thirteen and Furat was fifteen. He fell in love with her right away, sending her flowers and notes. At first she shied away from him, knowing her parents would never approve. But gradually she fell in love with him, too, and they began six years of quiet courtship.

Both families made loud and clear their objections to Dunia and Furat getting married. According to custom, Dunia's family was making arrangements for her to marry a cousin. She fought incessantly with her mother and brother when she refused to stay away from Furat. In 1999, when Dunia was nineteen, she told her father that under no terms would she marry anyone, ever, other than Furat. He finally relented and permitted her marriage to Furat.

After the ceremony, Dunia moved to Furat's village, where the couple lived in a one-bedroom home with Furat's parents and brothers. It wasn't an ideal situation for newlyweds, especially since the house had only a single mattress for Furat's parents, with everyone else sleeping on mats on the floor. Furat's family's disapproval of Dunia never faded, and Dunia was treated indifferently by her mother-in-law, Amal.

Despite these challenges, Furat and Dunia welcomed their son Yousif shortly after the wedding. Then came baby Teeba in 2002.

Then, as now, Dunia and Furat live in one of the most dangerous areas of the Middle East. Their village is in Diyala Province, a place that is fairly diverse in its religious and ethnic factions but has a long history of conflict between these groups. The explosion that killed Yousif and disfigured Teeba in 2003 was just one of many incidents of violence that surrounded this family and their neighbors on a daily basis.

That explosion started what Dunia calls her dark days. While Teeba endured forty excruciating days recovering from her burns in a Baghdad hospital, Dunia describes staying at Yousif's grave, wailing out a grief that seemed like it would never end. Yousif had been afraid of the dark, so Dunia lit candles for him every night.

Leaving his grave felt like saying goodbye to him for good, but after many nights she came to the realization that she had a daughter who was alive, still in the hospital, and needed her. So she said goodbye to Yousif, tore herself away from his gravesite, and returned to Teeba's bedside to care for her daughter through searing pain and inadequate medical treatment.

In the years after Teeba was burned, Dunia and Furat struggled to come up with the money to pay for Teeba's medicines—mainly creams that were effective only in softening the scar tissue and soothing her constant itching. All of their extra money went toward savings for Teeba's medical care. It was dangerous too. Once when Dunia and Furat went to a Baghdad hospital for Teeba's treatment, a bridge was blown up nearby and they had to run for safety, with Dunia holding Teeba under her abaya so she wouldn't see the dead bodies.

Shortly after that incident, Furat had to leave home to serve in the military, leaving Dunia alone to care for Teeba and their newborn daughter, Fatima—and to endure Amal's continued indifferent treatment. Dunia's family members did check on her from time to time, but she was left largely without support.

Dunia and her children saw American soldiers frequently after the collapse of Saddam Hussein's regime. Many of those soldiers were especially drawn to Teeba. She loved to dance and sing for them, and once they even took her for a ride in a Humvee. One time a doctor behaved aggressively toward Dunia when she took Teeba in for an appointment, but after Dunia managed to get away, it was American soldiers who escorted her home safely. The soldiers often helped her get through checkpoints on the way to doctor's appointments, and they would offer Teeba their American food, which she hated.

One soldier paid for Teeba's medicines when Dunia ran out of money at the pharmacy. He hugged Teeba and showed her pictures of his young children at home in the United States. He lifted her into his Humvee, gave her food, and offered to watch her while Dunia went to the pharmacy. When she returned, Teeba was sound asleep in the soldier's lap while he sang to her.

During her lowest times in Diyala province, Dunia dreamed of packing up herself and her children and convincing the soldiers to take her back to America.

On another trip to the pharmacy, a man bumped into Dunia, and the bottle of medicine she was holding fell to the floor and shattered. This man was a Christian, a Westerner who was married to an Arab woman. He quickly paid to replace the medicine, then struck up a conversation with Teeba and showed her a locket with his wife's picture in it. The man took a liking to Teeba, and after overhearing Dunia tell the pharmacist when she would be back, he returned at the same time with his own children.

That man asked Teeba if she was Sunni or Shia. "Neither, I hate them both," Teeba said. "I am a daughter of God." Everyone around them was stunned that a little girl her age would say such a thing. The man took off the cross he was wearing and gently put it around her neck.

"I am a Christian," Teeba announced to her mother as he closed the clasp of the necklace, and she tucked it under the neckline of her clothing.

But Teeba's delicate skin reacted whenever it came in contact with certain metals, so the necklace caused redness and irritation. Finally, Dunia convinced Teeba to take the necklace off, and she put it away in a safe place. The first night Teeba went to sleep without the necklace, she woke up screaming for her mother, and Dunia rushed to her side.

"The Virgin Mary is coming," Teeba said through her tears. "She wants to put a star on my chest and take me to someplace green."

These words scared Dunia—even though the Virgin Mary and Jesus are mentioned in the Koran, Teeba was only four years old and had never received formal religious training. She couldn't possibly have known about either of them.

The same dream kept returning for several nights. Thinking this was a sign that Teeba might die, Dunia privately prayed to Jesus and Mary to protect her daughter. "Please don't take my daughter," she pleaded in her prayers. "Take me instead." It was then she decided to return the necklace to Teeba, believing that perhaps she would be protected by wearing the cross. As soon as Teeba began wearing the cross again, the dreams stopped.

All of this reinforced a secret belief Dunia had held since Teeba was a baby—that Teeba had God's divine hand on her in a way that transcends religion. Not only could Teeba not have known about the Virgin Mary, she also rarely saw "green places" around her hot, dusty Iraqi hometown, where she was surrounded by nothing but sand and stone.

But our backyard is filled with tall trees, lush grass and flowers, with a golf course bordering our property, which could be exactly the green place Teeba saw in her dream.

Some people in the village judged her harshly for her choice to allow Teeba to leave for medical treatment, accusing her of selling her daughter to the Americans for money. The constant criticism left Dunia shattered like broken glass on the inside, even as she managed a steadfast exterior to her family and neighbors.

Just before it was time for Teeba to leave for America, Dunia realized that Teeba had lost the cross necklace. In a panic, she searched everywhere but never found it. She felt certain that the necklace was her daughter's protection, and that Teeba wouldn't be safe in America without it. She prayed to the Virgin Mary to protect her daughter, promising that if she ever had another daughter she would name her Maryam, which means "Mary" in Arabic. (The following year, Dunia gave birth to a daughter the day before Easter; her name is Maryam.)

The day finally came for Teeba and Amal to leave the village for Amman, Jordan, where they would stay with a host family until they could obtain visas to enter the United States. At five years old, Teeba couldn't understand why she was being taken from her home without her mother and sister beside her. She begged not to be separated from them. When it was time for final goodbyes, Teeba clung to her mother. Furat had to tear Teeba away from her mother's arms. She was crying, grabbing for her mother and her sister, begging to be permitted to stay.

Angry and confused, feeling abandoned, her final words to her mother were those of a child whose heart has been broken. "I hate you! You're not my mom anymore!"

With her heart breaking all over again, Dunia watched her daughter leave, not sure when, or if, she would see her again.

CHAPTER 13

HOMECOMING

Honey, I'm headed down to see Teeba," I said to Tim, who'd just settled down on the couch after a long day at work. I'd just gotten home myself, but had quickly changed and gotten a bite to eat before heading to the Ronald McDonald House.

That was our life in those days—both of us working full-time, driving back and forth from the Ronald McDonald House constantly, and driving Teeba to every doctor's visit and appointment. The Ronald McDonald House was about thirty-five minutes from our home, but no matter when or how I drove there, I always got slowed up by traffic. Sometimes I would bring Teeba and Amal home with me to spend some time together, then make the trip again to drop them off. But otherwise they were stuck inside the house, day in and day out. We tried to go to restaurants or on outings sometimes, but Amal was visibly uncomfortable seeing people showing bare skin, being boisterous, drinking, or displaying affection in public. They had only been here a month, and we were exhausted.

I gave the dog a quick hug, grabbed my purse, and headed for the door.

"Honey?" Tim called to me from the couch.

"Yes, what is it?" I said, poking my head back into the living room.

"I want to talk to you about Teeba and Amal," he said.

"What about them?"

Then he voiced what my own heart had been whispering: "Why don't we just bring them here to live with us? It would be so much easier on you, on us."

My heart surged, but I withheld the joy I immediately felt.

"Are you sure? Are you really sure?" I said, unable to suppress the smile growing on my face.

"I'm sure. Let's do it," he replied, his smile growing in response to mine.

I laughed out loud, jumped over to him, grabbed his neck, and kissed him. I'd been thinking about having them come to live with us for a while, but I needed him to come to that conclusion on his own. I had already disrupted our lives so much that I didn't dare ask yet another thing.

I called Huda on the spot and asked her to call Amal and let her know. The very next day I drove to the Ronald McDonald House, packed up all of their belongings, and brought them home with me. Teeba was thrilled, having plenty of space to spread out her toys, a big bedroom of her own, and a fridge full of food she could grab anytime. I assumed that Amal would be happy as well about the move—she now had a backyard where she could sit in privacy, a kitchen where she could prepare her own foods, and quiet time away from the busyness of the Ronald McDonald House. But as usual, Amal offered very little reaction.

Moving Amal and Teeba into our house was the right thing to do, but it plunged our home into chaos. We got a satellite dish that allowed Amal to watch some Arabic television, including Arabic soap operas and the news station Al Jazeera, so that Amal could remain connected to what was happening in Iraq. But the news back home was dire—violence continued to escalate, and the devastating events in her region of Iraq kept her in a daily state of panic. We also purchased calling cards that allowed her to make international calls, and nearly every day Amal dialed each of her ten children to hear the news from their village, shouting into the phone in Arabic. When she was upstairs in our guest bedroom, the sounds of her wailing and crying often reverberated throughout the entire house.

We understood why Amal was anxious and depressed. Life in the United States was incredibly fast paced compared to a small village. It also didn't help that Amal was surrounded by unfamiliar technology. One time she accidentally set off our home security system when she was alone, and I rushed home to find her in a panic. I'm sure the racket of the alarm must have sounded to her like some sort of warning siren she remembered from Iraq. I had to call someone to translate so that I could explain what was going on.

Amal missed her family, she missed her food, and she rarely had anyone to interact with who spoke Arabic. We tried to have friends who spoke Arabic come to visit when we could, but everyone had their own families, jobs, and lives. We were appreciative for any small amount of time they could spend talking with her or translating, but those were the only times she had someone to talk with.

One of those visitors was Leila, whom I'd met through a mutual friend and who became our regular translator and friend. Leila was Palestinian and spoke a different Arabic dialect, but she was able to facilitate basic communication with Amal and provide some connection to Dunia and Furat. Leila invited us over for dinner several times to enjoy meals of Arabic rice and okra in tomato sauce, along with tea with cardamom seeds and delicious spinach pies.

Even with someone like Leila generously giving her time to translate, the experience of facilitating a conversation between Teeba and Dunia was frustrating. I would get Leila on the phone, put her on hold to create a three-way call, then dial Dunia—only to find that she didn't answer or the connection had dropped. If Dunia called back, I would put her on hold and dial Leila, hoping she was available.

Plus, I was never quite sure during those conversations if everything was being relayed clearly to me, or if my emotions were coming across the way I intended. It was difficult to share personal or private feelings with a third party in the middle, especially when it was someone Dunia did not know. Still, I cherished those conversations with Dunia. I could hear the pain and anxiety in her voice, and I longed—no, I ached—to be able to communicate privately with her. To comfort her.

When Leila wasn't around, I always had English-Arabic dictionaries in my hand, purse, or pocket. I also kept a notebook close to me with familiar words and phrases written in Arabic. Many times I tried to act out the message I wanted to get across.

Like the time I tried to explain to Amal and Teeba what I was preparing for dinner. "Couscous! Couscous!" I exclaimed, shaking the empty box and pointing to the picture on the front. "With chicken!" I added, flapping my arms like imaginary wings, clucking and prancing around the kitchen.

Teeba and Amal stared at me for a moment, then burst out laughing. They kept on laughing until they could barely breathe, while I stood there and watched them, confused. It turned out that "cous" in English sounds exactly like the Arabic word for a private part of a woman's anatomy. It wasn't often that I heard Amal laugh, but that one had us all laughing until we cried.

Despite all these challenges, Tim and I tried our best to give Amal a positive experience of American life. We took her shopping to buy new clothes and shoes. When Halloween rolled around, we got Teeba dressed up in her princess gown to go trick-or-treating, and we even got a crown for Amal, who joined us as we went house to house. She told us about a similar holiday in Iraq, during which children go door-to-door collecting candy and money, though not dressed in costumes.

We took Amal to the dentist for the first dental cleaning she'd had in fifty-two years of life, and to the doctor for a physical. We also hired a tutor to help Teeba and Amal learn English. Amal resisted, but Teeba absorbed the language quickly and was fluent within a few months.

Language became a flash point between Teeba and Amal. "I know

English and you don't," Teeba often told her grandmother when they argued.

Bringing Amal and Teeba into our home made them more isolated than ever. Tim and I hoped the Arab-American community in Cleveland would step up to welcome them, take them to the mosque, or just come for visits. While they were at the Ronald McDonald House, it was easier for visitors to drop by. But once they moved in with us, the visits dwindled. The majority of the Arab-American community lives on the west side of Cleveland, at least thirty-five minutes away from our home, and it became inconvenient for many of them to make the trip.

There was a cultural barrier as well—many Middle Easterners living in the United States are from large cities or were educated in the West. Amal, on the other hand, had minimal education, was from a poor rural village, and had never been to a large city other than periodic trips to Baghdad. The divide between her and other Arab-Americans in Cleveland was almost as wide as it was between her and us.

In October of that year, we got word that a Cleveland-area mosque wanted to organize a fund-raiser for Teeba; they invited her, Amal, Leila, and me to attend. It was Ramadan, and the fund-raising event was in keeping with the Muslim custom of *Zakat*, an offering to the poor and suffering that often occurs during that holy month. *Zakat* is a token of thankfulness for all God has given us, and for His giving Muslims the strength to complete their month-long fast.

I found myself feeling nervous as we were driving there. I had mixed feelings about visiting a mosque. Because of my faith as a Christian, I know that it is not for me to judge those who are different from me. In fact, it's the opposite—I knew it was my duty as a Christian to be welcoming, open, and loving toward people different from me, following the model of how Jesus lived His life. I thought often of this Bible verse during that time: "Do not judge, or you too will be judged" (Matt. 7:1).

But the mosque visit still had me uneasy. The customs of the Muslim faith and culture were so foreign to me. Plus, we were at war with Iraq at that time, and Iraqis, Muslims, and Middle Easterners in general were not well understood or accepted—at least not in my world. For many Americans, life in the Middle East was little more than something we watched on TV but never really connected with, even when we heard on the news about our American soldiers or innocent Iraqis like Teeba and her family being injured or killed.

Most of what we heard about Muslims was tied to radical groups, but I just couldn't accept what we'd heard now that I was developing this con-nection to Teeba and her family. Through Teeba's and Amal's eyes I was now seeing the personal plight of the Iraqi people—how millions on the other side of the world had the same desires, goals, and dreams for their lives and their families as we do here. As I learned more about Dunia's life back in Iraq, my eyes were being opened to a world I'd never before imagined.

When our little group arrived at the mosque, Teeba was ushered into a back room to play with the other children, who—as often happened—all immediately stopped what they were doing and stared at her. As usual, I was uneasy about leaving her with strangers, and she was initially timid as well. But it never took long for her to join in on the fun with other kids.

I covered my head with a hijab, left my shoes outside of the sanctuary, and knelt in the back with the women while the men knelt on rugs at the front during the service. The men were comfortably and casually dressed, while many of the women were completely covered but for their faces and hands. Watching the clear separation between men and women at the mosque and how they dressed compared to me was unnerving.

The service was mostly in Arabic, so I couldn't understand any of what was happening. But the repetition of the prayers sounded so melodic, echoing off the walls of this enormous room. It was empty except for the worshippers, with vaulted ceilings, a rich red-and-gold carpet, and an ornate crystal chandelier hanging in the center of the room.

At the conclusion of the service, a collection was made that totaled

$2,000 for Teeba's care and expenses. Some of the women brought the envelope to Amal. Their conversations in Arabic were friendly but brief. I stood to the side, struggling to restrain my urge to go around the room hugging and kissing everyone to show my appreciation for their generosity toward Teeba and Amal. It was clear that my physical expressions of gratitude would make them uncomfortable.

I hoped that some of the women might have offered to stay in contact with Amal, or even visit her in our home. But that never happened, and Amal became more and more isolated.

As Amal became more agitated and fearful in our home, Teeba became more comfortable. Even a simple trip to the grocery store was an adventure, and she relished a long, hot bath in our jacuzzi tub filled to the top with bubbles. She didn't like American food at first, but she came to love McDonald's hamburgers with french fries and chocolate shakes. She also became quite fond of putting nail polish on Tim, eating warm pita bread with sautéed eggplant, and wearing anything with princesses on it.

Oh, and she loved her new wig! Teeba and I returned to Jeffrey's salon, accompanied by Maria, Carla, and Leila, about a month after her fitting to pick it up. We once again made our way back to his private room and Teeba climbed back up into Jeffrey's salon chair, just as she had the previous month, but a little more confidently this time. She'd gotten all dressed up for the occasion, in a patterned skirt, blouse, and white shoes with black bows.

"Look what I have for you!" Jeffrey said, presenting the dark blond wig to Teeba ceremoniously.

She seemed hesitant at first, averting her eyes while Jeffrey applied the wig tape, slowly put it on her head, and trimmed the long front into bangs that covered her scarred forehead.

"Look at how beautiful you are!" I exclaimed.

She finally looked up to gaze at herself in the mirror, and mixed emotions played across her face. It was almost as if she got a little shy, not recognizing herself. But gradually, you could see an uplift in her confidence. Her chin rose and her smile grew firm. She looked beautiful.

"Thank you," she said in English, as she walked out with a broad smile on her face and confidence in her step.

But the process of applying a wig—especially one that will stay put on the head of a busy child—isn't easy, and we would have plenty of tearful mornings calling Jeffrey because Teeba just couldn't get it to go on the way she wanted it. It was made of real hair, but it didn't entirely look like or behave the way hair growing from her own scalp would, and at five years old Teeba had a hard time grasping that. It was bittersweet.

She couldn't have what she really dreamed of—hair—but this was the next best thing.

Even though I'd never anticipated becoming so involved in the life of this little girl, I was fully committed to loving and caring for her for as long as she was with us. We never looked too far ahead—we just moved ahead one day at a time, never getting wrapped up in the days, weeks, or months to come.

But privately, deep in my soul, I was already praying and hoping that she would be allowed to stay with us forever. When I would wake up each morning to this tiny fragile child and look into her big, brown, and soulful eyes, I felt that each day my old life was peeling away and a new life was crystalizing. Life as I had known it prior to July 16, 2007, was quickly fading away.

While at first we were Mama Barbara and Papa Tim, that didn't last long. Just a few weeks after she came to live with us, she asked her parents in one of their phone conversations if she could call us Mom and Dad. They said yes, and from that day we became one big extended family— divided by language, nationality, geography, and faith, but united in our love for Teeba.

CHAPTER 14

THE FIRST SURGERY

Tim and I woke up on the morning of September 5, 2007, feeling frantic. It was like someone was squeezing my insides.

"Honey, it's time," Tim said, touching my arm gently when our alarm clock went off. He didn't need to. I had barely slept and was already wide awake, worrying.

"I feel like I can't even breathe," I murmured. "This is going to be such a hard day for Teeba."

I was already struggling not to cry, and I wasn't even out of bed yet. But Tim and I knew we had to put on our brave faces for Teeba. I headed upstairs to her room to wake her at 6:00 a.m. with a soft kiss on the forehead and a gentle stroke of her hair. She was so tiny against the king-sized bed, surrounded by pillows and stuffed animals.

"It's time to wake up, honey," I said, trying to be calm and soothing, not wanting to do or say anything that would give her cause for alarm. "It's time to go."

Today was the day that Teeba would go to Rainbow Babies & Children's Hospital to have her first set of expanders inserted. It wasn't actually cold that day, but I was so chilled from anxiety that I wrapped

Teeba up in a little bathrobe with a hat and warm socks, also grabbing her Hannah Montana blanket and Binti Shatra. Holding Teeba, I climbed into the back seat next to Amal, who was stoic as usual. Teeba snuggled into my neck as we headed out into the dark morning, picked up Leila, and drove to the hospital in silence.

Outwardly, I made my voice quiet and calm, but my inner voice was praying loudly and voraciously: *Please, God, take the burden of these surgeries off of Teeba. Put her pain and suffering and fear on me instead, Lord. Let me have her burned and scarred skin, God, and allow her to have mine. As she fasts out of necessity for this surgery, we will fast by choice so that we can suffer beside her on this day.*

After the long year we spent trying to get Teeba here, we were now taking that first step toward making her beautiful, as she had so innocently asked Dr. Gosain to do during our first meeting. This was the first step toward healing the scars of her past.

To prepare Teeba for this moment, we'd met a few days earlier with a child-life specialist at the hospital named Catherine. She was friendly and calming, and she explained to Teeba what would happen on her surgery day, while Leila translated. Catherine gave her little blue pajamas to arrive in and even a tiny little doctor's hairnet. Teeba got to pick the scent of ChapStick that would line the mask for anesthesia, see the operating room, and feel the hospital gown she would wear. She also got to pick the movies or TV shows she wanted to watch as she recovered. Catherine even gave her a fabric doll that she could use as her "patient," performing all of the surgical preparation tasks on her—putting the pulse oximeter on the doll's finger, getting an IV, and placing an anesthesia mask over the doll's mouth.

She did this on me at home, too—we would "steal" surgical gloves and tongue depressors from Dr. Gosain's office during her appointments, then I would be her "patient" at home. She looked deep into my eyes, examined the back of my throat, squeezed my arm with her hands as if she were checking my blood pressure, and pretended to check my heart with an imaginary stethoscope.

But now it was time to do it all for real.

In this first surgery, Dr. Gosain would place two tissue expanders—one on the right side of her neck and another on her back. The expander on her right neck would create new skin to be advanced, or stretched, to partially replace the scars on that side of her face. The expander on her back would create enough new skin to replace most of the scar tissue on her forehead.

As part of her preparation for the surgery, Teeba had also gotten the chance to see the expander itself, which was a rectangular balloon made of silicone measuring 6 centimeters by 8 centimeters—about 2 1/4 by 3 inches—attached to a small hose with a port. That port would become the entry point for the saline that would be injected into the expander once a week. When fully expanded about five months later, the neck expander would hold 200 cc of saline (about 6 3/4 ounces) and the back expander would hold 290 cc (nearly 10 ounces).

Leila had come along to support us and translate so Teeba and Amal could understand what was happening each step of the way. Leila had also helped us reach Dunia and Furat the previous night so we could update them on the surgery to come. Together, we did our best to communicate what the first surgery would entail. I could feel the terror in Dunia's voice, knowing she couldn't be there to soothe her daughter's pain.

How do you comfort someone you don't share the same language with? All I could do was cry with her.

In the pre-op room everything was just as Teeba had asked for it to be—*Dora the Explorer* was on TV, and Teeba was dressed in her hospital gown with little animal characters. Without any doctors or medical equipment nearby, Teeba was calm and smiling as she watched Dora head out on her animated adventure. I crawled into bed next to her; Tim sat at the end of the bed rubbing her feet. Leila and Amal stood nearby.

Teeba's calm didn't last long. As doctors and nurses began entering the room, her smile faded.

The first step was to take her blood pressure—easy enough, I thought. But even though Catherine had showed her what it would be like, Teeba recoiled as the cuff began to squeeze her arm.

"It hurts, it hurts!" she said in Arabic, alarm rising in her voice. "Take it off *now!*"

Then came the pulse oximeter, a small clip-on device that went on Teeba's finger to measure the oxygen level in her blood. Now Teeba's panic began to escalate, and she clung to my arm, crying. Amal was on the opposite side of her, trying to talk to her and clearly embarrassed by her outburst, but Teeba pushed her away. Leila was doing her best to comfort both of them and explain what was happening in Arabic while I did the same in English. I tried to help the nurse to control Teeba enough that she could do just these basic tasks.

But none of it helped.

"I need some help in here!" the nurse called through the open door as Teeba began to scream and flail her tiny body around the bed.

More nurses came into the room and leapt into action. They surrounded her bed, each trying to restrain Teeba as she struggled against their grips. Behind the nurses, Amal and Leila continued to shout at Teeba in Arabic, trying to get her to calm down. She grabbed for me, clung to my neck, and wouldn't let go. Even though she was only thirty-two pounds, the nurses were no match for her sheer terror. They tried giving her a liquid sedative in a tiny cup to relax her, but she shook her head hard and continued to scream.

"Teeba, it's okay, honey, it's just going to help you fall asleep," I said, trying to keep a soothing tone in my voice over the chaos of the room, as I choked back tears.

My eyes caught Tim's, who was watching this entire scene with a look of helplessness in his eyes. I felt equally helpless and paralyzed by a mixture of fear and panic. I had seen those awful pictures of how the tissue expanders would deform her body. I pictured them removing her damaged skin to replace it with new. I knew this was just the first step of years of pain and terror for her. I wanted to rescue her from this. I had to fight back the urge to say, "Forget it! We changed our minds!" and bundle her up and take her back home. But I couldn't. There was no turning back.

The original plan was to roll Teeba back into the operating room, deliver the anesthesia, then start the IV after she was under. As they moved her to the gurney, she was still sobbing uncontrollably and clutching my hand.

"Would you like to walk with us into the operating room?" one nurse asked tensely, seeing how tightly Teeba was still clinging to me. "It might make it easier for her."

I let go of Teeba just long enough to put on the surgical gown they gave me, then reached for her again, walking beside her holding her hand as they rolled her back. But all the preparation Catherine had given her and the cherry ChapStick she'd selected to line the mask didn't mean a thing when she saw that anesthesia mask coming at her face.

Teeba screamed with a force that didn't seem possible for a child her size, and she spiraled into a full-blown panic. I was sick with fear for her, looking around at the scary medical instruments, beeping machines, and doctors and nurses in masks, and imagining how frightening this must be for her. I had to step away as the doctors and nurses restrained her again to put on the mask and administer the anesthesia. Gradually, her flailing faded and she finally drifted off to sleep.

I begged them to let me stay with her.

The nurse looked me in the eye. "No, you need to wait outside," she said, gently but firmly escorting me out of the operating room.

As I walked out, Tim was there waiting for me. I fell into his arms sobbing, the kind of sobs that hurt your throat and make you want to vomit. I pressed my nose to the window hoping to get one more glimpse of her, but Tim held me tightly and escorted me back to the waiting room, where Amal and Leila were waiting, along with my friends Maria, Terri, and Carla. I kept thinking how horrifying it would be to be in a foreign country, surrounded by doctors who don't speak the same language as you, experiencing a painful surgery, all at only five years old without your parents nearby.

Seeing Teeba so terrified had shaken me to the core. That wasn't the last time I would ask myself: *Are we doing the right thing?*

About two hours later, Dr. Gosain came through the waiting room door, and we all jumped to our feet. He said the surgery had gone well, and he explained what the next steps would be. It seemed the crisis for that day was finally behind us.

We were wrong.

Teeba's eyes gradually fluttered open.

Tim and I stood by her bed in the recovery room. Her neck and back were wrapped in gauze where Dr. Gosain had inserted the expanders.

Teeba's eyes looked right, then left, and she started to remember where she was. Her face transformed from restful calm to sheer terror, and she escalated within seconds into sheer panic. She started screaming, trying to fling herself out of bed and tearing at her hospital gown. She managed to get it off and rolled to the floor—now naked, writhing and screaming on the ground. In English, she yelled "I'm hot, I'm hot!" and "Untie me! Untie me!"

I was confused. We were trying to hold her and comfort her, but she wasn't in restraints. But then it hit me—she'd been only nineteen months old when she was burned, but she must be flashing back to those forty days she'd spent in the hospital in Iraq. They probably had to restrain her to keep her from touching her scorched face, and now this deeply held memory was springing to the surface. *Oh, God, how I wish I could take this pain away from this child!*

Modesty being such a central tenet of Muslim tradition, Amal was horrified by Teeba's nakedness. She knelt on the floor beside her, desperately trying to keep Teeba's body covered even as she squirmed and screamed. Amal was yelling at her in Arabic, but it was hard to tell if she was reprimanding her or trying to be compassionate. She hadn't cried a single tear. I tried my hardest to convey to Amal not to worry about

Teeba's modesty in a moment like this. These doctors had seen all kinds of things with children. We needed to be calming and comforting to her.

Teeba had somehow acquired Herculean strength at that moment, and it took several of us to get her back into bed, where she continued to writhe. My dear husband—six feet, four inches and so strong and dependable—looked fragile at that moment. I wanted to also comfort him, but we could only look across Teeba's bed at each other, exhausted with despair. He told me later that this was the moment he truly fell in love with Teeba, watching this poor fragile child so panicked. He'd become just as attached to her as I had, but the emotion he felt in that moment was a punch in the gut.

After more than thirty minutes of tears and terror, I was finally able to get Teeba to settle into my arms in a rocking chair next to the bed. At one moment she seemed soothed by me singing and talking to her, then the next moment my voice was intolerable to her. In the end, she just wanted silence. And to be held.

So that's where we stayed for more than three hours, just rocking back and forth.

Amazingly, Teeba was able to go home on the same day as the surgery, in spite of everything that had happened. Tim and I tucked her, exhausted, into her bed at home to recover. As emotionally grueling as that first surgery was, I knew the worst was yet to come.

It wasn't long after the insertion of the expanders that the expansion process began. Each week we went to the hospital, where the nurses would inject a saline solution into the ports to start gradually filling the expanders and stretching the skin. This wasn't painful to Teeba, but she could hear and feel the saline as it traveled by her ear on its way to the expander on her neck.

Only ten days after that first surgery, the unthinkable happened. The port site for the expander on her neck began to swell and took on a yellowish cast. It didn't seem to hurt her, but it looked like the skin was tearing. I rushed her to Dr. Gosain's office and learned that the expander was ulcerating, or breaking through the skin. Her skin had become necrotic, meaning that the tissue at the point of the tear was starting to die. It took on a purplish black color.

That meant Teeba had to go back in for another surgery to remove the necrotic tissue, which brought along with it all the same anxiety and screaming when the anesthesia was administered. And all the same screaming and writhing on the floor post-surgery. And all the same soothing and rocking until, finally, Teeba fell asleep.

Dr. Gosain removed the ulcerated tissue but kept the expander in, which should have solved the problem and allowed the tissue expansion process to continue. But then we got more devastating news—her cultures came back indicating that Teeba had a serious infection around the area called pseudomonas. It's caused by a common bacteria; in fact, healthy people can carry this bacteria around without knowing it or having any problems. But it is commonly spread in hospitals, where people who are weak or ill—including those with burns—are more susceptible to the serious and even deadly infections it causes, which are often hard to treat with antibiotics.

Three steps forward, four steps back. Less than a month after her first surgery, Teeba was back in the hospital for her third surgery to remove the expander in the right side of her neck and the infected tissue around it. That meant expansion on that side of her face had to wait until the skin was fully healed.

Surgery didn't get any easier for Teeba the third time around. Every time the anesthesia was administered, she panicked and had to be restrained and sedated. Every time she came out of the anesthesia, she flailed and screamed and pulled at her IVs. As her English quickly improved, I could at least communicate with her without a translator, but she still couldn't communicate her frustrations to me.

"Please no, Mom!" She would plead with me before the doctors administered the anesthesia. "Why, Mom? I hate you, Mom!"

But as the sedatives and anesthesia did their work, and she came close to succumbing to sleep, she always said the same thing: "I'm sorry, Mom. I love you, Mom." Then her eyes would close.

That third surgery brought what might seem like a small blessing, but felt like a major victory.

When Teeba first arrived in America, she had warts all over her fingers. She hated them because they made her burned hands look even worse. I had made an appointment with a dermatologist to have them removed the week after her third surgery. But just a day after Teeba started the antibiotics that would kill any remaining pseudomonas infection, she came running downstairs.

"Mom! Mom! Look!" she called in English, splaying out her fingers. "Gone! Gone!" The warts had disappeared, literally overnight. We were able to avoid having them burned or cut off. This was huge for Teeba.

After a month of disappointments, it was a small but much appreciated miracle.

CHAPTER 15

TEEBA: MEETING DR. GOSAIN

I remember sitting in Dr. Gosain's office on the day that he described his recommended treatment plan. Huda was doing the translations for my grandmother, and they were far too complicated for me to understand. I could tell my grandmother was upset, but I didn't care. I had no cares at that point because in my mind I was giggling and thinking, *I'm going to be beautiful again!* Naïve and innocent, my mind was running around and my stomach was jumping, but my ears weren't listening.

It wasn't until after the appointment that my grandmother told me what the next few years were going to be like for me. Even so, the concept of "years" wasn't something I was able to grasp. I told her my *baba* ("father") said we would be back in a few weeks. I was still smiling inside at the thought of being beautiful.

Many of my memories of visits to Dr. Gosain's office include having cameras in my face taking photos of my progress, having meltdowns over something as simple as getting my blood pressure taken, and sitting for hours in the waiting room. I really hated going to the doctor when I had my expanders because I disliked receiving the solution through a needle into the "bubbles," as I called my expanders. The solution was cold, and I could hear and feel it going from the tip of the needle to my neck, back, or chest, depending on where the expander had been placed.

Still, it was better than the memories I had of going to the doctor in Iraq. The doctors there were not always trustworthy; many times they put my family through unnecessary pain. Doctors and hospitals stressed my parents out and drained their money and energy. The doctors were impatient and grabbed me without caring if they were being gentle or not.

But the bright spot in those early days was my new wig. I couldn't wait to get my hands on it. When Jeffrey put the sample wig on my head, it was so soft and realistic, nothing like I had expected. My mom bought me a black wig one time in Baghdad that was synthetic and cheap—all we could afford. It was so itchy and irritating that I ended up only wearing it once or twice. But this wig did not burn or itch my scalp, and it fit my head so much better.

Even though I desperately wished I had hair, I had accepted that my only choice would be to settle for a wig.

CHAPTER 16

A HOUSE IN CHAOS

As I sat in the waiting room during Teeba's first surgery, I tried to pass the time by checking a few emails. Waiting there for me was a message from Mahmood, the relative of Furat's who spoke English and had helped with our earliest contacts with Teeba's family. I'd sent him a message the night before, asking him to pass along an update to Dunia about the surgery plans.

He responded in broken English a few hours later:

> Thanks Barbara for the update. I'm sorry that I could not respond to your queries promptly. Actually the situation in Teeba's village escalated, but please keep this secret and do not tell Amal the grandmother.
>
> Unfortunately Amal's son [Ahmed] has died, a sniper has shoot him. Please, please do not let the grandmother neither Teeba know about this. Their village has become a hot spot and therefore both grandmothers for Teeba have fled their village including Teeba's little family.

Recently I came to know that Teeba grandmother's house (the other grandmother who still in Iraq, it is the mother of Teeba's mother) was on fire and maybe has completely destroyed. . . . Again do not tell Teeba and grandmother about this situation.

I was stunned. But with Amal sitting just across from me, I couldn't let my shock be apparent on my face. I reread the email a second time, then tried to act casually as I handed the phone to Tim. He read it, then just looked up at me in silence, also trying not to react. He passed my phone to Leila, who passed it to Maria. We all sat shocked, trying not to betray our emotions to Amal.

So, as we took Teeba home that day, emotionally drained from our grueling time at the hospital, I was also weighed down with the burden of this terrible secret—hiding the news of Ahmed's death from Amal. Suddenly the tragedies of daily life in Iraq didn't seem so far away. It was right here in front of me; a woman whom I'd welcomed into our home and referred to as "sister" had just lost her beloved son to unspeakable violence.

Teeba's family was now our family, and the thought of any of them being hurt, killed, tortured, or kidnapped became too much to bear. This tragic event was on my mind every time I looked at Amal, but I knew that her family was right—it was their place, not ours, to tell her at a time when she could be surrounded by the comfort of her husband and other children. But we had no idea when that time would come.

As Amal sat in her bedroom every day endlessly dialing her husband and each of her children, she became more and more agitated that the only person she couldn't reach was Ahmed. Every time she spoke to another one of her children, they always made an excuse for why she couldn't reach him—saying that his phone was lost, or he was working, or the connection was bad. Between watching Al Jazeera and her phone calls home, every day Amal was hearing bad news about the escalating violence in her hometown. Given that and her worries that her husband would take another wife in her absence, her anxiety continued to ratchet up. Her five-times-a-day prayers became louder and more fervent.

It was painful to watch her so tormented, knowing the truth that one of her deepest fears—losing a child—had come true.

Amal was sensitive about allowing Tim and I some privacy. She often tried to prevent Teeba from being with us in the evening, but that was our favorite time with her after a long day at work. Teeba has always loved to dance, and her favorite show at the time was *Dancing With the Stars*. She'd jump up on the couch and cuddle with us, admiring the dancers.

One evening, Amal came down to the living room where we were watching TV, and she demanded that Teeba go with her upstairs. Teeba looked at us with imploring eyes and pointed to the TV. She clearly wanted to stay and watch the dancers. She'd quickly learned the word *no* in English, and made it clear that she wanted to stay with us and keep watching the show. But Amal wouldn't tolerate such disobedience. She hauled Teeba up by the arm and forced her up the stairs and into her room.

Moments later, I heard screaming. Tim and I leapt off the couch and ran up the stairs to find Amal disciplining Teeba. This was while Teeba had partially stretched expanders in her neck and back.

"Om-Nazar!" I screamed, using her more formal name, meaning "mother of Nazar," her eldest son. She stopped and stared at me. "No! Stop it! She has expanders!" Teeba sat on the bed sobbing, and I ran to her to comfort her.

I grabbed my cell phone and dialed the number of the woman who had translated for us at the airport. I explained the situation to her and then put Amal on the phone. They talked briefly. After she hung up, Amal backed off but offered no real response, while I attended to Teeba to be sure that there was no damage to her expanding skin.

It was a moment when I knew I was crossing a line, stepping into the middle of Amal's discipline of her granddaughter. Coming from such a matriarchal culture, Amal was surely offended by my interference. We never truly knew how she felt about this admonishment, but the physical discipline never happened again.

Teeba's arrival had attracted a lot of media attention. That was intentional on my part—I knew getting and keeping our story out there would create supporters I could call upon when needed. I also wanted to have people who could publicly come to Teeba's defense if the government or some other entity tried to force her to go back to Iraq.

But the flip side of all the attention was that complete strangers regularly showed up at our door to give Teeba gifts, having seen her on TV or read about her in the newspaper. One family we didn't know drove from Erie, Pennsylvania, two hours away, with their daughter who had Down's syndrome. They'd seen Teeba on TV, and their daughter wanted to meet her at Christmastime. Cheerleaders from a local high school had a tiny uniform made for her, and they invited her to cheer with them at a football game. If we were out to breakfast, there were times when total strangers would pay for our check. All of this was a shocking display of kindness and generosity that Tim and I were not used to. It was very humbling.

One evening, I received a call from a man who identified himself as an Iraqi living nearby who had read the story about Teeba's arrival. He wanted to come over that evening and bring her a gift of a guitar. I told him yes, but after I hung up, the call left me a little unsettled. About an hour later there was a knock on the door, and I opened it to find a man in his fifties of Middle Eastern descent dressed in jeans, a US Navy hat, and dark glasses, with a guitar in hand. Teeba was thrilled with her gift— she promptly asked for guitar lessons—but our visitor was vague about who he was and why he wanted to visit; he simply said Teeba's story had touched him because she was from his home country of Iraq.

This man told us his name was David, and how proud he was of his son, then serving in the US Navy. David had worked for the United States in Iraq in what he called an "undercover" capacity, remaining quiet but always listening. He said he was born and raised in Iraq and had suffered under the regime of Saddam Hussein, but he didn't provide many details. He appeared to be sensitive to the plight of women in Iraq, and he told us he had no problem putting a gun to a man's head whenever he encountered someone harassing a woman.

He had plenty of questions about Tim and me, but he wouldn't answer any questions about himself. After chatting with us for a while, David sat down to talk to Amal. The two had a rapid conversation in Arabic for ten or fifteen minutes, then he turned to us calmly and said in English: "The grandmother has to go. Teeba must stay here."

"What? What do you mean?" I wasn't sure how to respond. It raised my suspicions immediately, but I wasn't sure who to be suspicious of. Did David have some ulterior motive? Was Amal not being forthright with me? The language barrier had me constantly guessing whether I was getting the whole story. What weren't people telling me? Were my questions being translated properly?

"I know how women are treated in that tribal culture," David replied evenly. "Teeba's life will be better here. She needs to stay."

He then returned to his conversation with Amal while Tim and I sat there, dumbfounded. It was pure speculation on our part, but Tim and I came to suspect that David may have been sent by the US government to check out what was going on in our house. We'd publicly brought over these two individuals from Iraq, a country with which the United States was still at war. We had people of Iraqi descent in and out of our home constantly, and we were regularly making international calls to a part of Iraq outside of US control. We thought we were just a normal suburban couple living outside of Cleveland who'd tried to help an injured little girl from the other side of the world, but to some, I'm sure what we were doing raised suspicions.

After that first visit, David stuck around for a while in our daily comings and goings. He called me regularly and offered to help us with translations, but he always avoided the camera. I attempted to do research on him but couldn't find a thing. By this time I'd started to meet some members of the Arabic community in Cleveland, but even among them David was virtually anonymous.

After a few months, I'd finally had enough of David's enigmatic presence in our lives. I called him and asked him to meet me for breakfast at a restaurant near my house. He showed up, as usual, in his US Navy hat and dark aviator sunglasses.

We sat down at the counter, exchanged a few pleasantries, and David launched into his typical list of questions about us: "How is Teeba? How are the surgeries? Have you talked to her family?"

"You've asked me a lot of questions, but when I ask you questions you never answer them," I said. "I won't answer any more of your questions until you tell me who you are and why you're here."

David laughed lightly. He'd always given us the impression that he had to be secretive because of the work he did for the government. He threw me a bone with a few irrelevant details from his life, and we spent the rest of our breakfast engaged in nothing more than small talk.

But I never got the answers out of him that I was seeking, so as I paid the bill and said goodbye, I knew that it would be our last conversation. We never heard from him again.

November came. The temperatures started to fall and the snow began to fly. Stress and pressure from her family finally became too overwhelming for Amal, and Ahmed's death was taking its toll on her husband and other children.

David had been part of one phone call in which Furat had begged Amal to come home.

"Teeba's safe there, you can leave her with Barbara and Tim," Furat told Amal. "But you need to come home."

Teeba was in the room listening to the conversation, and I know that she understood what her father was saying. She was stoic, not reacting to it in the moment, but I learned later how much that broke her heart. She thought her father didn't want her to come home. And in truth, he probably didn't. He knew that she was getting the care she needed here, and that she would be safe from the violence of their village. With expanders in place and her medical treatment just getting underway, sending Teeba home with Amal—even just for a temporary visit—was not an option. After a year of trying to get her here, I knew it would be next to impossible to get her back into the country to finish her surgeries if she left.

One of our last evenings with Amal was Thanksgiving. I'd put up my Christmas tree and all of my decorations for the big Thanksgiving dinner I hosted every year, where we'd get as many as thirty people stopping by. On that night we opened our doors to any friends and family who wanted to join us.

A few nights before Thanksgiving, Tim ran out on some errands to get ready for the holiday. With Tim gone, it was one of the rare times that Amal removed her hijab and let her long dark hair, streaked with gray, flow freely. She came out of her room and into the kitchen, watching with fascination as I began my three-day process of brining turkeys in giant coolers, which would be followed by another day of drying on cookie sheets, then stuffing the underside of the skin with garlic, butter, and fresh parsley.

"Amal! Amal!" I called out when I saw her, motioning in my direction and pointing to the turkeys. "Come, help me!"

Warily, she pulled up the long, draping sleeves of her abaya. She took the wooden spoon I offered to stir kosher salt into the icy water, where the eighteen-pound birds would soak for the next twenty-four hours. I pantomimed grabbing the turkey under the wings and moving them to coolers.

"Ready?" I nodded at Amal as she grabbed the other side of the turkey. She smiled back.

While Teeba snapped pictures and giggled, Amal and I hoisted the slippery bird out of the sink. Staggering over to the cooler, we attempted to ease it gently into the frigid water. Instead, it slipped out of our hands and splashed into the water. Our clothes and hair were dripping wet, and all three of us were laughing hysterically. It was my last wonderful memory with her.

A few days later, Amal left to return home. We expected that day would be an emotional one for Teeba, so we chose to say our goodbyes at home instead of at the airport. All of the adults cried, me in particular knowing the horrible news of her son's death awaited her when she arrived home. We armed her with notes written in English that she could use if she needed help, particularly during her connection through Chicago.

While Tim and Nasr, Leila's husband, drove Amal to the airport, Teeba and I made brownies and played with her dolls. Our home settled into peace immediately, and we all started out on a new and uncertain path.

What do you do all day with a five-year-old girl from a foreign country who's without her parents, still learning English, and undergoing long-term medical treatment?

That was the question Tim and I faced once Amal had left. Both of us were working full-time and enjoying every moment we could with Teeba, relying on friends and family to help with her care when we were working. She was at an age where she couldn't just sit around all day—she needed to be in school and spending time with other children. But because she was in the United States under a medical visa, she wasn't permitted to attend a public school.

Thankfully, Carla introduced me to Tina Turk, who owned The Goddard School—a private daycare and preschool near our home. I scheduled a meeting with Tina, once again clutching the stack of newspaper articles and photographs I brought whenever I was planning to ask for help for Teeba.

Tina didn't need much convincing. "Absolutely, I would love to help Teeba," she said, even offering to take her on free of charge.

But allowing Teeba to come to her school wasn't the same as admitting any other child. We didn't have signed parental consent to enroll

Teeba, we didn't know her vaccination history, and we didn't have any of the documents Tina would normally require from a parent. At the time, I didn't even have power of attorney to make significant decisions on her behalf. I was eventually able to get her birth and immunization records and have them translated from Arabic, but it was not a quick or easy process.

"We're going to make this work," Tina said. "I'll get it all worked out."

So that's how I found myself standing in front of a class of prekindergartners, all sitting attentively on a rug, while holding a handful of photographs of Teeba. "Children, this is Mrs. Marlowe, and she's here to tell you about a new friend who will be joining our class, whose name is Teeba," said Tina to the class. "She has some pictures to show you as well."

All fifteen pairs of eyes swiveled to stare at me.

I sat down on the floor with the children and introduced myself as "Teeba's mom." Any other way of describing myself would have been too much for them to comprehend. I began to tell them how I had read about a special little girl in Iraq who had an accident. I opted for the word *explosion* instead of *bomb* to describe what happened, not wanting to scare them.

"Sadly, her older brother died and Teeba was terribly burned," I told them, as they looked back at me, startled and solemn. "But guess what? We are able to help her! She's going to have lots of doctors' appointments and surgeries. Right now she doesn't speak English very much, but maybe you could help her learn?"

I passed around pictures of Teeba so that they'd be prepared for her appearance when she came to the school—I didn't want Teeba to be a surprise in any way.

"She looks different, but she's just like all of you," I said. "She loves to run and play, and she's very sweet."

The children listened and asked questions, but amazingly, very few were about her burns. They were more excited and curious about the prospect of having a new friend.

"Does she have brothers and sisters?"

"Where is her mom?"

"How many surgeries will she have?"

Then they ran off to their next activity, and Tina and I smiled at each other. This was really going to happen!

That night I told Teeba all about what I'd seen at the school, all the new friends she was going to make, and what her teachers would be like. She'd never been to school before, but she didn't seem afraid or fearful. It was just another new experience in a long list of them she'd had during her short time in America.

Just a few days later, I dressed Teeba in a green-and-navy plaid dress with black velvet trim at the neck, sleeves, and bodice, paired with little black shoes with straps. She wore her dark blond wig, and the expander in her neck was clearly visible above the neckline of her dress. It was November, but it was warm enough that day that she was able to wear her pink bug raincoat with eyes that rolled around and antennae that stood erect on top of the hood. I had packed her lunch of pita bread, cucumbers, apples, and carrots—along with a piece of candy—in her pink princess lunch bag.

As we arrived at The Goddard School, we walked into Mrs. Heather Robinson's class holding hands. Incredibly, the kids ran to greet Teeba as if they had known her forever. Even so, I was reticent to leave her. I stood and watched her for a little while but knew I had to pull myself away. After I left the room I watched the door close behind me, expecting her to come dashing out, afraid to be left behind. But it never happened. Peeking through the oblong window beside the door, I could see that not only were Teeba's eyes not searching for me but she was already engaged with her new friends.

With the accepting hearts of children, the class welcomed Teeba as a friend right away. The kids didn't shrink back from her appearance or seem afraid. They all gave her cards they'd made to welcome her, and in circle time said things like "I'm sorry you were burned," and "How was your flight?" She taught them to say tafaha ("apple") and by then had learned it in English too.

Within a day or two, it was as if the other children didn't even see

Teeba's scars or her growing expanders. She was another kid, just like them. For her part, Teeba loved school and we had our new morning routine, singing the Barney song—"I love you, you love me, we're a happy family"—and learning her right and left by memorizing the directions to school.

It wasn't long before she was making friends, having sleepovers, and taking swim and tennis lessons. The three of us settled into a new daily routine of school, work, doctors' appointments, and playdates. I loved walking her into school and seeing her scamper off with her friends. I loved being able to see the new pictures she'd drawn at the end of each day. Having never been a mother, I was for the first time seeing things through the eyes of a child. It became our new normal. We had become a family, and I loved her as I would a daughter. In my heart, I felt like I had become Teeba's second mother.

But I still tried to hide that feeling away. I couldn't give myself permission to think of myself as her mother. She had a mother, one who was painfully missing her, who wished she could be the one to take her daughter to school and longed to be there during her surgeries. Every fun and joyous moment we spent with Teeba was tinged by a painful one for me— feeling guilty that I got to have those moments with her and Dunia didn't.

I also knew that when her surgeries were over she would have to go home, and I would experience the pain of saying goodbye to a girl I had come to love so much. I couldn't imagine that future pain, yet I knew it was a fraction of the pain Dunia was enduring being so far from her daughter. I was never able to fully live in the moment because Dunia was always there with me, in my gut and in my heart. Every moment with Teeba was bittersweet.

CHAPTER 17

GRAFT DAY

E ven after Teeba recovered from her pseudomonas infection, the right side of her neck still wasn't healed enough to replace the expander on that side. Instead, Teeba had another surgery in October—her fourth in less than two months—to have a new expander placed, this time on the left side of her neck to create skin for that side of her face. Surgery number five followed in November after the port malfunctioned in the expander in her back.

As the temperatures dropped, Teeba's expanders continued to grow, giving her the appearance of having a large tumor on her neck and a hunched back. Once a week, we took her to Dr. Gosain's office at Rainbow to have saline injected into her expanders. We would sit in the waiting room, surrounded by children with all kinds of medical conditions. It was difficult to see so many children crying and anxious or playing with toys, anticipating when their name would be called.

The expansion process wasn't too bad. Dr. Gosain or his nurse Randi would gently cradle the expanded skin as they injected the saline, and the medical photographer, Apryll, regularly stopped in to document Teeba's progress. Dr. Gosain always made us feel like Teeba was the only patient he had. As gentle as he was, he was clearly calling the shots, even as Teeba fussed or resisted or tried to negotiate her way out of something uncomfortable.

"No!" Teeba said when Dr. Gosain or Randi was about to inject the saline. *No* was one of the first words she learned in English, not all that much different from the average American kid.

In those early days, Teeba's expanders had internal ports, meaning that Dr. Gosain had to pierce the skin in order to inject the saline into the port. She'd start squirming and fussing as soon as they put the numbing cream on the injection site. She wanted to be the one to choose when the needle went in, which wasn't easy for a doctor to accommodate when he had the next patient waiting for him. Sometimes they played along with her drama for a while, but in the end Dr. Gosain always had a way of softening her tough shell.

Dr. Gosain was short in stature but strong—he had been captain of the wrestling team at Harvard University. Sometimes Teeba would try to arm wrestle him, but he would pick her up and spin her around like she was a feather. He allowed her to speak her mind, but he always set her straight. Teeba clearly loved challenging him. He became a member of our family.

No trip to Dr. Gosain was ever complete without Teeba thrusting her hand into the basket of stickers at the nurses' station. Carefully studying her options, she'd pick out a few every week—stickers of princesses and superheroes and animals of all kinds that would start in my purse then end up stuck to the windows beside her car seat on the way home. Before Teeba, my car was spotless. Now, the windows were covered in stickers and there were Cheerios and french fries all over the floor.

Eventually we were able to do the injections at home. Teeba was proud of the fact that she was later able to inject the saline herself, and even let a friend do it a few times. As the expanders grew, she would tell me they felt heavy, and the expander on her back made it difficult to sleep. But for the most part, Teeba was able to do many of the same things as other kids. We had some fun with the process too—sometimes we would decorate the expanders with stickers as a surprise for Dr. Gosain before appointments. Or, with a fresh layer of lipstick, I would plant a perfect imprint of a kiss on the expanded skin on her neck. If any kid ever made a nasty comment about her expanders, I told Teeba to tell them that there was a monster hidden inside them that would jump out and eat them if they didn't cut it out.

As I cuddled Teeba at night, I would stroke the skin over her expanders and we would talk about treating them with great respect. These were the precious, delicate pieces of skin that would soon form her new face.

Meanwhile, on the other side of the world sat a mother who worried day and night about her daughter's surgeries but was unable to come to her bedside. She could not draw her child into her arms as she cried or kiss away the tears that clung to her cheeks. Her face was not the last one her child saw before the anesthesia pulled her under, nor was it the first one her daughter saw as she returned to consciousness. She could not look the doctor in the eye and ask him her most fear-filled questions, but instead had to rely on translations of secondhand information. Her daughter was thousands of miles away, in the care of people she'd never even met.

I couldn't begin to understand Dunia's pain at being separated from Teeba during her surgeries. Reaching her by phone was difficult and required scheduling calls when a translator was available. Despite unreliable phone connections and the language barrier, the pain I heard in Dunia's voice tore my heart out. I was sitting in the place she should have been—beside Teeba, holding and comforting her through her pain and fear.

But I didn't give up on maintaining that connection. Some people questioned why I was so insistent on it. The longer Teeba was with us, the easier it would have been to lapse in our communications with her family in Iraq. Life was hectic—weekly calls could have become biweekly, then monthly.

I couldn't do that. Not after everything Dunia had been through. I never lost sight of the fact that this was *someone else's child* that I'd been entrusted with.

We called Dunia as often as we could to give her updates and consult her when we had to make medical decisions. We relied heavily on Leila to convey updates to Dunia, especially during surgeries. I also wanted Dunia to talk to Teeba as much as possible. Unfortunately, being around other Arabic-speakers so infrequently, Teeba gradually began to forget her Arabic. Soon we even needed a translator present for her to speak to her mother. Sometimes we would have to force Teeba to talk—even if it was in English—or sing a song, just so that Dunia could hear her voice. Sometimes Dunia and I would just cry together or make kissing noises into the phone—anything to create a feeling of intimacy and closeness.

But there was one word that all of us understood, no matter what our native language—*love*. Sometimes that was all that really needed to be said: *I love you.*

It was April 28, 2008, and the day was finally here.

Teeba's back expander had been in place for nearly eight months, and her left neck expander for nearly six. It was time to attempt the first skin graft. This would be an eleven-hour surgery that would start with Dr. Gosain excising the expanded skin on her back, removing the expander, and stitching up the incision. That flap of skin that the back expander created was just the right size to cover her forehead from ear to ear and from her wig line to her nose.

Before the surgery Dr. Gosain created a template of Teeba's forehead that he could use, much like a sewing pattern, during the surgery, attaching it to the skin flap and then marking the exact line that he would cut. To achieve the kind of smoothness he needed for forehead skin, Dr. Gosain planned to spend hours meticulously picking any fatty tissue out of that skin flap with tweezers before suturing it to Teeba's forehead.

The expander on the left side of her neck had created a skin flap large enough for the left side of her face. That portion of skin would be "advanced," meaning the expander and the scarred skin would be removed, and the skin would be stretched upward and sutured to existing tissue higher on her face. Actually, we were killing two birds with one stone—this procedure allowed Teeba to have a root canal to deal with an infected tooth at the same time.

That morning we went through our normal surgery-day routine—up early, dressing Teeba in her little blue pajamas, and to the hospital by 7:00 a.m. We were more anxious for this surgery than the others, knowing that Teeba's burned skin was actually going to be removed. It was terrifying and exciting at the same time, knowing she would soon have new, smooth skin on her face.

Even though this was Teeba's sixth surgery, things had gotten no easier. She knew what was coming with the anesthesia and, like a typical six-year-old, tried every delay tactic in the book. With panic rising in her voice, Teeba agonized over the decision of which arm the IV should go into and tried to negotiate to delay the anesthesiologist. She insisted on having the doctor do a countdown to a predetermined number before inserting the needle. She absolutely hated losing control of the situation. When she could avoid it no longer, she clung to me for dear life, huge tears rolling down her face.

"No! Leave me alone!" she yelled at the nurses and doctors, ordering everyone to leave the room. "No sleepy! No sleepy!"

Once again, the doctors and nurses had to hold her down to administer the anesthesia, even while she pleaded with them and me to stop. Staying with her until the very end had become part of our routine, so I suited up in a surgical gown and returned to her side, grabbing her hand tightly and trying to do something, anything, to soothe her.

"Mommy, why are you doing this to me?" she sobbed. "I hate you!"

I walked beside Teeba's bed as she was rolled into surgery, still holding her hand and looking into those terrified eyes until the moment they closed. As always, before she drifted off, Teeba said, "I'm sorry, Mommy.

I love you so much." Her pressure released on my hand and the gurney continued on without me.

As always, when I turned to walk away, Tim was there to catch me just before my knees buckled. Sobbing so hard I could barely catch my breath, I watched her through the operating room window for as long as I could before Tim helped me back to the waiting room.

We settled in for a long wait alongside what people came to call Team Teeba—the entourage of people who were always there to support us, including Leila, Maria, and Carla. As I watched Tim read and eventually doze off, I wished I could sleep too. I did my usual pacing, crying, praying—then repeat. As usual, I'd come with my Kindle, magazines, and a pillow, but I couldn't concentrate on anything. I just sat there, staring at nothing or staring at everything.

We were always given pagers when we checked in for Teeba's surgeries. We never strayed far, but it enabled us to take a walk around the hospital or go down to the cafeteria. One of the nurses—and on rare occasions, Dr. Gosain—updated us periodically from the operating room. Those updates were much appreciated, but nothing could calm our frayed nerves until we saw her.

On the day of the first graft, I stepped into the small chapel to pray for a few minutes. *God, please give me some reassurance that we are doing the right thing for Teeba. She has so much physical and emotional pain ahead of her. Please bring peace to her mother's heart. Guide the hands of the doctors and nurses, and bring her through this surgery and recovery safely.*

I think God probably wanted to put in earplugs to block us out, we were so fervent in our prayers.

Finally, after hours and hours, we got a page that Dr. Gosain wanted to speak to us. We headed up to one of the family conference rooms.

"Teeba did a good job," he began.

I always found it odd when he said that, since I knew she was asleep for the whole procedure—but it gave us some relief. Dr. Gosain was direct and to the point, explaining what he did and what we could expect when we saw her. That was an endearing quality. He knew we wanted to get to her bedside immediately.

Tim and I stood up, ready to see her new brave little face. I gave Dr. Gosain a big hug with tears streaming down my face. Tim and I thanked him, then we locked arms and headed toward the recovery area in the ICU. We walked slowly, anxious to get there but afraid to look.

As we came around the curtain pulled by her bed, we saw Teeba, still asleep and lying tiny and frail atop the adult-sized hospital bed. Both Tim and I froze in our tracks, and my hand flew up to my mouth.

Teeba's face had been ravaged. Starting by her left ear, a thick, swollen incision line snaked across her cheekbone, dipped down beside her puffy lips, and finished just below her chin. It was a bulging divide between her mottled scars and the smooth new skin that now covered her jawbone. A lightweight cap covered her forehead, where the new skin from her back had been sutured. Her eyes were black and blue and swollen shut. Her head was swollen to the size of a bowling ball, with tubes sticking out to allow fluids to drain from the incision sites and to prevent swelling. One tiny foot poked out from under the blanket.

Tim and I were in shock. We couldn't take our eyes off her face.

"Oh, Tim," I sobbed. "Oh, our dear Teeba. What did we do? What did we do to her?"

Sobbing himself, he held me tightly as we sunk into chairs the nurses had positioned by Teeba's bed. We were speechless. As difficult as it was to see her face like this, I felt just as terrified anticipating what was to come once she emerged from the anesthesia. All we could do was hug each other and cry.

"She can't see you like this," Tim whispered to me, gently rubbing my back. He was right. We pulled ourselves together just enough so that we could be a source of strength and comfort for Teeba when she woke up.

We knew what was coming.

As Teeba gradually became aware of her surroundings, she began the flailing and screaming that had become part of every surgery, pulling at her hospital gown and trying to rip out her IVs. In her medical records, the nurses used terms like "agitated," "irritable," and "uncooperative." But those words don't even come close to explaining how hysterical she was.

I felt helpless. Nothing I could do would take away her pain and fear. So I did the only thing I could, the thing I did after every surgery—I gathered her up in my arms, held her tight in my lap, and rocked her in the chair next to her bed as she screamed. This time, as in the past, Tim could do little more than watch, looking fragile and defeated. I wished I could comfort him too.

After hours of rocking, Teeba began to settle, and I placed her gently back in bed and climbed up beside her, holding her in a fetal position. I was desperate to comfort her, to make her feel calm and safe. I was afraid to move, afraid to breathe for fear of waking her. Around us, I could hear machines beeping, the shuffle of feet and conversations in the hallways among nurses and other patients. I just wanted quiet. I wanted enough quiet that she would sleep through any pain or discomfort. Quiet enough so she'd sleep and sleep and bypass all that awaited her in recovery. Quiet enough that she could avoid seeing herself in the mirror until she was fully healed.

These were unrealistic dreams.

For the next four days I lived at the hospital 24/7, wearing the same T-shirt, sweats, and slippers. I rarely left Teeba's side; in fact, it was hard to even go to the bathroom because she didn't want to be left alone. I don't even remember showering or washing my hair. Teeba always wanted me to sleep with her, and I never wanted to let her go. I'm tall and that bed was tiny, but I spent the nights snuggled up next to her while she slept. I was desperate to sleep but rarely did.

Teeba was constantly restless and agitated, tugging at the pulse oximeter and blood pressure cuff. One minute she'd want to lie down, then the next she'd want to walk around—she just couldn't get comfortable. Tim came every day to sit on the bed and rub her tiny feet, and he would race out to get whatever she asked for. Even if she wanted chicken nuggets, french fries, and a chocolate milkshake from McDonald's at 3:30 a.m., Tim would go get it. It was never too late or too far for him to get anything for her.

I sustained myself on coffee and little boxes of assorted cereals and snacks from the coffee station on the recovery floor. Teeba and I watched nature shows together to pass the time, and one particular program must have stuck in her brain. It showed a mother bird chewing up worms for her young, then placing the regurgitated food in their mouths. As I held a bucket for her while she vomited after surgery, she looked up at me, worried: "Mom, am I going to have to eat that?"

Night after night, day after day, Teeba demanded that I wheel her around the hospital hallways in her wheelchair, bundled in blankets and pillows with Binti Shatra tucked by her side. I would push her wheelchair and drag the IV poles for what seemed like hours until I thought I might collapse. On every nighttime walk we stopped in one room that was trimmed in floor-to-ceiling windows. There we could watch the lights of the cars zipping by below and look up into the clear, star-filled night. I would sit and gather Teeba up on my lap and gaze at the sky, imagining Dunia thousands of miles away looking at those same stars, worried and afraid for her daughter.

On May 2, we finally got the green light to take Teeba home so she could begin the long healing process. Once home, she would stand in front of the mirror looking at her badly bruised and swollen face—so severe we worried that it would never go away—and gingerly touch the bandaged areas.

Finally, one day, we found her standing in front of the mirror wearing a huge smile and touching the new skin on her cheek and forehead. In those small patches of smooth, unscarred skin, she was finally seeing progress toward the end result. It was such a relief to see that after so many setbacks we had finally taken a step forward.

I moved behind her and smiled back at her reflection. It was a glimmer of hope, and we all clung to it, knowing we still had a very long way to go.

CHAPTER 18

"MY BROTHER AND YOUR MOTHER SENT ME"

D o you know about the night stealers, Mom?" Teeba asked me one
night in a hushed voice.

"No, what are night stealers?" I asked.

"They come into your house at night and steal you and put you in a
bag," she replied, her face deathly serious.

We were lying side by side, nose to nose, in her bed, blankets pulled
up to her chin. Nighttime was when Teeba would open up. She would say,
"Mom, I'm scared. Can you come sleep with me?"

The stories she told me weren't just the product of a child's imagina-
tion. They were memories of a life in Iraq that no child should ever have
to experience. That particular story about the night stealers never fully
made sense to me until I learned later from Amal that a man once came to
their neighbor's house holding a black plastic garbage bag, and inside was
the severed head of one of her children. Even when Teeba and her family
were sleeping, she told me, they were never fully asleep. They were always
on alert for the bad guys who might come for them.

She remembered only rarely leaving her house or walled-in yard and always keeping the gates closed to keep the Iraqi soldiers from getting into their house. If they did see soldiers, she recalled her family having to put their arms straight out at their sides so the soldiers could check them for weapons. Her stories weren't all about violence though.

"One time I fell into the river by my house," she told me another night. "There was a crocodile and he almost got me before our neighbor pulled me out!"

Around Teeba's village the bad guys often dressed as policemen. So she was terrified the first time she saw a police officer in the United States. She was in the car with Tim and Maria's husband, Gary, when a police car pulled up beside them—a shirtless suspect was in the back. Teeba shrank back in fear, clinging to Tim's arm. Fearfully, she told him about the policemen in Iraq who would take people away.

I saw an opportunity to fix that particular problem one day as Teeba and I were leaving the dentist's office. There was a police car parked next door, and I drove over and pulled up beside him.

Teeba panicked. "No, Mommy, don't talk to him!" she said, clearly anxious about being so close.

I assured her everything would be okay as the police officer got out of his car and approached my window. She sat in her car seat and stared at him with wide, terrified eyes. I explained to the officer who Teeba was and shared her fears about policemen. He looked at her for a moment and then, in his gentlest voice, told her that the police in America protect children and make sure they are safe. He explained that if she ever felt afraid or threatened and saw a policeman, she should call out or run to him.

This interaction with such a caring police officer seemed to alleviate Teeba's fears, although it still took a while for her to accept that in the United States, policemen are the good guys.

One night shortly after Amal left, Teeba and I were snuggling in bed. Every night I would hold her close and use my index finger to trace the outlines of her facial features. Her eyes would flutter and she'd fall asleep under my touch. It was one of my favorite parts of our bedtime ritual for the longest time.

On this night, Teeba asked me in her still-broken English, "Mom, how come you never had any kids?"

It was a knife to my heart. The truth was too much for a six-year-old to hear—my anguish at always wanting children and my hysterectomy. My years of staying silent about my pain as I watched other families spending time together. Before Teeba came, I sat in church one Sunday behind a family with a daughter who was about three years old. Her mother was holding the child close, and the little girl reached up her tiny hand to stroke her mom's face. She looked down, locked eyes with her daughter, and whispered, "I love you." It was such a sweet moment, but it also punched me in the gut with pain.

Now I was having some of those same moments with Teeba. I'd squashed down that desire in myself for so many years, right up until I saw that photo of Teeba in the newspaper the previous year.

I simply responded: "Well, honey, God had other plans for me. You know how I like to do things to help animals."

"If you had kids, would you have wanted a little boy or a little girl?" Teeba asked.

"I always wanted a little girl," I said, hugging her a little tighter and planting a kiss on her forehead.

Her response caught my breath: "Don't you know?" she asked sweetly. "My brother and your mother sent me to you to be your daughter."

I was dumbfounded. I stared at her, speechless. Both my mother and Teeba's brother Yousif had died in 2003. Losing my mother was a pivotal moment in my life. We had a difficult family life when I was young, but later in her life we discovered a relationship that I wished we'd always had. It was Tim's encouragement in part that helped us to grow closer later in her life, and I'll always be grateful to him for it. I came to see her wonderful spirit and the true person she was—a good woman who'd endured her share of hardships.

Since Teeba was still learning English, I'd never shared anything with her about my mother. There's no way she could have known about her.

I choked back my tears until after I'd tucked Teeba in and left her room that night.

That night was one of the many times that I began to see God's divine hand on this little girl. We experienced these "God moments" with Teeba over and over.

One day she was flipping through a book of animal pictures when she stopped abruptly on one page. She turned the book toward me so I could see it and pointed: "This is my favorite." It was a ladybug, which my mother had loved and collected. One year we even got my mother a birthday cake in the shape of a ladybug. One frigid January, the day after my mother died, my sister Karen and I saw a ladybug ambling along her kitchen wall. It's unheard of to find one in the extreme cold of a Cleveland winter. We knew that it was Mom reaching out to comfort us.

Now, out of all of the dozens of animal pictures in the book, Teeba chose the one that most reminded me of my mother.

"Do you know what that is?" I asked her.

"No, I just like it," she responded, and kept flipping through the pages innocently while I gaped. Karen and I often talked about how much our mother would have loved Teeba and enjoyed spoiling her. My mother once worked at a shoe store, and Karen and I laughed together thinking about her picking out the perfect shoes for Teeba.

Another time, I spotted Teeba lining up her Barbie dolls in a row. Barbies were a particular favorite of girls in Iraq, and she'd received many as gifts from our friends since the day she arrived.

"What are their names?" I asked.

She went down the row, pointing: "This one's Sarah. This one's Anna. That one's Sarah. That one's Anna." Every single doll had one of those two names, which were the names of my two grandmothers. At one point in my life I'd been closer to them than to my own parents, but they had both passed away years ago. There's no way Teeba could have known about them.

She watched me, puzzled, as I burst into tears. "How do you know those names?" I said.

She shrugged. "I don't know. I just like them," she said, and went back to playing.

To Tim and me, these "God moments" comforted us and reassured us that we were doing the right thing by Teeba. Still, we went to bed every night emotionally spent. Inevitably one or both of us would wake up in the middle of the night filled with anxiety. The more we fell in love with this little girl, the more fear consumed us in those hours of insomnia. They were the same fears we'd experienced from the moment she arrived. *Will she be able to stay? Will her parents want her back? This isn't our child; what right do we have to keep her here?*

The language barrier always made it difficult to know what Dunia and Furat were really thinking, so I never could be sure how they truly felt about Teeba being with us and staying long enough to complete her surgeries. In my heart I felt that Teeba was my daughter, yet I had to respect the fact that she had parents who I knew loved her.

All of this was an emotional roller coaster that never ended. We never had moments of security when we felt sure Teeba would still be with us one month, two months, or even a year from now. We lived our lives in small batches of time. We dealt only with the situations in front of us, thinking no further than a few weeks or a surgery at a time. I even used sticky notes on my bathroom mirror to keep me focused only on the next step.

When a crisis arose, we called a family meeting with our closest friends to talk things through and decide what to do. When people asked us about events that were two or three months in the future, we simply couldn't answer. We stayed perpetually in the moment, and every day seemed like a step of faith.

When you don't have children, your life is always organized. At least mine was. There were no fingerprints, scuff marks, spills, or scratches in my home or car. Wherever I left something, it was always in the same place later.

Enter the Iraqi whirling dervish. This little girl turned everything in my home inside out and upside down. In addition to all the dolls and toys given to her as gifts, Tim and I constantly lavished her, joyfully and willingly, with all the things little girls dream of. She had an art table, a huge dollhouse, Polly Pockets with all the accessories, and her own lounge chair. Her closet was packed with clothes and shoes. Toys and dolls were piled up everywhere, with me forever trying to keep things organized. It didn't work.

Our friends Sue and Mike Miller could tell how frazzled all this disorganization was making me. Sue's family owned a construction company, and both of them knew how to build just about anything.

"I sure wish Tim and I had that kind of talent," I grumbled one night as we had dinner with Sue and Mike. "I'd give anything for our basement to be finished so I could move all these toys down there and give Teeba a nice place to play with her friends."

A couple of weeks later, Sue and Mike announced they were giving us a gift—they were going to construct a play area for Teeba in our basement—and a special room for me and my kitchen supplies, with lots of shelving and a wrapping station. I'm not speechless very often, but I was at that moment. I wept at their generosity.

Soon, lumber and drywall were being delivered and measurements were being meticulously made. Sue and Mike worked tirelessly for weeks and weeks while still keeping up their full-time jobs. They built a wheeled stage in the playroom to allow Teeba and her friends to perform dance recitals and musicals for us. Off the playroom they created a "dressing room" for their performances. I painted the walls with pink and pale-green stripes, and I installed a whiteboard for playing school, a flat-screen TV with a Wii, and assorted beanbags and other furniture to make it the perfect place for Teeba to hang out with her friends.

To say we were grateful wasn't enough. Sue and Mike did more than restore our house; they made it a home for this precious addition to our family.

Soon Teeba and her friends were dressing up in princess costumes, hats, and accessories, admiring themselves in the full-length mirror, and creating dance routines and musicals. Teeba's first girlfriend, Maggie, lived down the street, and she took part in every one of Teeba's plays and elaborate Hannah Montana concerts. They spent hours together playing with Barbies and Polly Pockets.

This was our new life, and I loved every minute of it.

So did Tim, reliving all of those same joyous moments he'd shared with his older children. He read books to her, taught her to read, and used flash cards daily so she could learn basic math skills. He taught her how to ride a bike and allowed her to paint his nails and dress him up with her costume jewelry. He spoiled her rotten and never missed an opportunity to tell her how proud he was of her and how much he loved her.

To this day, I'm amazed to think of how my husband went along with my crazy notion of bringing this little girl from the other side of the world into our home, then embraced her as if she were his own daughter from the beginning.

CHAPTER 19

ENDURING STARES

When are you going to get *it* out of here?"

The father of one of the little girls in Teeba's class stood in Tina's office at The Goddard School, pointing an accusing finger in Tina's face. He'd asked her for an after-school meeting to discuss some concerns, and that "concern" turned out to be Teeba.

It wasn't the first time that a parent had come forward with worries about Teeba being in their child's preschool classroom. A few parents had worried that Teeba, being from a third-world country, might have brought diseases to which their children would be susceptible. Other parents were made uncomfortable by the questions their children were asking about why it was so dangerous in Iraq. One little boy's father was a member of the US military deployed to Iraq, and his mother worried that he would reach the conclusion that his dad was hurting little kids like Teeba.

But this went far beyond practical concerns.

"That *thing* is scaring my daughter," continued the angry father, still waggling a finger in Tina's face. "That thing—that girl from Iraq. *It's* scaring my daughter and I want *it* out of here."

Tina was taken aback, but she didn't miss a beat.

"She's not *it*. Her name is Teeba," Tina said, calmly yet firmly. "Maybe you could come visit the classroom sometime and meet Teeba. If you can show your daughter that you're not afraid of Teeba, then maybe she won't be either."

He was silent for a moment. "Quite frankly, I think it's hard to look at," he said angrily. "And I want *it* out!"

"I'm sorry you feel that way, but this is a five-year-old child, not a 'thing,'" she said, keeping her cool despite the anger rising in her. "She's not going anywhere."

"Are you choosing her over my daughter?" he roared.

When I learned later about her response, it made me love her all the more: "I'm not choosing anyone over anyone," Tina said. "She's staying. And your daughter is welcome to stay as well."

Fuming, the man stalked out of Tina's office, slamming the door behind him. He withdrew his child, and Tina never saw him or his daughter again. That was the last time she got a complaint about Teeba's presence at the school. For the rest of the children and their parents, Teeba was just a regular kid, expanders and wig and burns and all.

Outside of her school walls, however, Teeba got plenty of stares. Some of the children in our neighborhood refused to play with her. Kids would point and say, "Look at her face!" It was even worse when she had expanders in—people assumed she had some enormous tumor on her neck or back.

One Halloween, at a time when she had expanders in, Teeba dressed up as a witch and was having a great time running around with her new friends. I walked the streets with her and her friends, smiling at the way they ran up to each different house. But then I saw Teeba walking slowly away from a particular house, her shoulders drooping and tears brimming in her eyes.

"What is it, honey?" I said. "What's the matter?"

"I want to go home," she said, even though everything had been fine just a few minutes before. I finally got out of her what had happened. The adult who opened the door had said, "Wow, your mask is so scary!"

But Teeba wasn't wearing a mask.

Often those kinds of situations made me more angry and upset than Teeba. I would try to run interference, deflecting her attention away from their stares.

"You don't have to do that," she told me once. "I know they're staring."

How she was able to handle all the stares and comments always left me astounded. Her attitude toward life, even at that young age, truly amazed me. Her glass was always more than half-full. When people stared, often she would just flash them a big smile and the world was good.

For the most part, the United States has reached the point where those with disabilities are not treated differently than anyone else. If someone is in a wheelchair or has a missing limb, their disability is easy to see and understand.

Burns are different, though. They pull the skin tight in different directions, with some sections of tissue looking white and others a red brick color. Some burn scars are tough and thick, and they can pull the eyes, nose, and mouth out of alignment. Plus, surgeries to repair burns can often cause scars in other parts of the body where skin has been removed and grafted. Burned skin distorts a person's features so much that people stare just to figure out what kind of trauma that person endured. The expanders on top of everything else just magnified the number of looks Teeba got from curious strangers.

The longer Teeba stayed in the United States, the more stares she got for good reasons. Because of all the media attention, she got recognized everywhere we went.

For example, soon after Amal left, while Teeba was in her first round of tissue expansion, I got a call from *People* magazine. They wanted to do a feature story on us for their "Heroes Among Us" section. The writer and photographer came out to spend a few days with our family and document our lives with Teeba. Most kids would be shy about strangers following them around, snapping pictures and asking questions. But not Teeba. She had expanders in at that time, but she opened up to the camera in a way the photographer, Ron Haviv, said he rarely saw in children—especially children with injuries.

Ron captured so well the feature that drew me to Teeba in the first place—those dark, soulful eyes. Ron had been on assignment in Iraq multiple times, including to Diyala Province where Dunia and Furat lived. We got to know him over those three days he stayed with us, and he is still a close friend today.

Shortly after the *People* story came out, the floodgates opened and we started getting calls from producers of various talk shows. The only one we said yes to was Dr. Phil. It was the only one I felt comfortable with. But his producers were mostly young and inexperienced, and they had all kinds of crazy ideas about wanting to bring Teeba's family here from Iraq for a big surprise reunion on the air.

I tried to patiently explain that the United States was at war with Iraq, so the immigration issues between our two countries were complicated. It took me a full year to bring Teeba here to get medical treatment, so it would be virtually impossible to obtain the visas necessary to bring her family here. It would be emotionally difficult for Teeba, who had been in the US less than a year and was right in the middle of long-term medical treatments. She'd finally started to settle into a routine after a chaotic first few months. It was just not the right venue to have that kind of a reunion. I don't think most of them really got it.

I remember when I sat Teeba down to talk about it. "Honey, do you know who Dr. Phil is?"

"No, who's he?"

"Well, he's a man who has a TV show in California," I said. I used a voice that made it clear to her that something exciting was about to happen. Her eyes got wide.

"And we're going there to be on his show!" I exclaimed.

She squealed and jumped around in excitement, even though she had no idea who Dr. Phil was or what a talk show was. All she knew was that maybe if we went to California and were on TV, she would get to meet her favorite star, Hannah Montana.

Teeba had already become a bit of a fashionista, so the first important decision she focused on was what to wear for her TV debut. She was six, but she was still so tiny. Unfortunately, her back expander was so large that we had to find clothes big enough to fit over it that weren't huge everywhere else. She settled on a pair of black leggings with lace on the bottom and a pink and black silky shirt.

Teeba was terrified to fly, and as we were scrambling around the house on the morning we left, she wouldn't budge from the stairs, sobbing about having to get on a plane. But once we boarded, Teeba was treated as a special guest, which distracted her from her fear of flying. She got all kinds of extra attention and goodies from the flight attendants, but she was most excited by her window seat. When we landed, the show's driver pulled up in a massive black Escalade with blacked-out windows, to which Teeba pressed her face the whole way to the hotel, anxious to get her first glimpses of California. The driver came back for us in the morning to take us to the studio, where we got a tour and were ushered into our own personal dressing room filled with refreshments, a TV, comfortable chairs, and a couch.

While we waited, people flowed in and out of the room—producers, hair and makeup people, and a woman whose job was to care for child actors and make sure they were getting their education and were treated fairly. She was there to help entertain Teeba while we went out on stage alone, to be followed by Teeba after a commercial break. Leaving her with strangers always caused me anxiety, but Teeba had everyone laughing and smiling as soon as they came in the room.

On set, Dr. Phil ran a video of Teeba's story, then brought Tim and me out to interview us about our journey. After a commercial break, Teeba paraded out holding the hand of a producer, and the audience burst into a standing ovation. She was a little intimidated by the applause, crawling up on the couch next to me and snuggling into my shoulder. Dr. Phil shook her hand and introduced himself, but she had no words.

"How did you learn English so quickly?" he said to start the conversation.

"I don't know," she said, shrugging.

"What other languages do you speak?" he asked, probably suspecting she would say Arabic.

"Well, I'm trying to learn Spanish," she said in her tiny voice, and everyone laughed.

"I know you like Barbie," he said. "So I called her and she sent you a letter."

She narrowed her eyes skeptically at him, trying to determine if he was telling her the truth.

"Here, can you see it?" he said, holding the letter out in her direction.

"Well, I can't read it!" she said, once again getting the laughter of the audience.

In the letter, "Barbie" said she was proud of Teeba's bravery and was sending her some special toys. Then out came two women pulling two wagons brimming with toys—including every variety of Barbie toy and two American Girl dolls, one of which looked like Teeba with long hair and brown eyes. Teeba was taking karate lessons at that time, so they'd outfitted the doll in a karate outfit just like hers. And just when it couldn't get better, out came one of the producers riding in a motorized Barbie Jammin' Jeep Wrangler.

As she stepped into the miniature Jeep holding onto her karate American Girl doll, Dr. Travis Stork, who was just launching his spinoff show *The Doctors*, said, "Teeba, you'll have to drive your car back to Cleveland."

"I can't," she said with attitude. "I have to take an airplane."

Once again she had the audience laughing. But our Hollywood adventure wasn't over. Dr. Phil announced that the Dr. Phil Foundation was setting up an account for Teeba, and he encouraged viewers to contribute. He also offered the three of us a vacation to Riviera Maya, though it wasn't possible for us to make the trip given her surgeries and limitations with Teeba's visa.

And then the dramatic finish: "Tonight, Teeba," said Dr. Phil, "you are having dinner with Ariel and all the princesses at Disneyland."

By then, she was completely overwhelmed with all of her gifts, and now the idea of dinner with the princesses! After the show, the driver returned us to the hotel to change, then took us to Disneyland. Teeba couldn't wipe the smile off her face as she got lots of extra hugs and special attention from the Disney princesses and had her picture taken again and again. She perched on Tim's shoulders as we watched the parade, then stopped by Mickey's house before it was time to return to the hotel for our final night in California.

The next day, as we walked through the airport to head home, we were recognized from the *People* story, and strangers would stop us to applaud Teeba's bravery and wish us luck. Teeba beamed. Just six years old and barely in the United States nine months, and she was totally comfortable in her own skin—even when it was burned and expanded.

About 99 percent of the responses we got from all the media attention were positive. There was an outpouring of support for Teeba and genuine expressions of love and caring. But the attention did bring criticism, as well, including people who thought we were keeping Teeba away from her family and should have sent her back. When our story was published in a local magazine, one commenter wrote: "Although this story is sweet, Teeba has a mother. I can't imagine how painful it would be to see my child call another woman 'mom.' She is not the Marlowes' child."

When Teeba was in first grade, the father of one of her school friends approached me at a school function and handed me an article about Middle Eastern children living in the United States.

"They should all go back where they came from," he sneered, spewing hateful words about the Iraqi people.

I lost it, right there in the hallway of Teeba's school.

"You have a lot of nerve," I spat back, unable to control the anger in my voice. "Your daughter is friends with Teeba. You don't have to like me or my husband or approve of our decisions, but you cannot, under any circumstances, be nasty to my daughter. I don't give a damn what your opinion is."

Then I turned on my heels and stormed out of the school.

All of that paled in comparison to a reaction we got when our story was posted online by our local newspaper. One person wrote in the comments section: "Why don't you help someone from this country? She'll just go back to Iraq then return here and blow us all up!"

I usually don't react to any of the online comments about our story, whether they are good, bad, or indifferent. But this one made my blood boil. He didn't know me, my background, or what I'd done or hadn't done. Yet here he was, readily indicting an innocent little girl who had committed no offense whatsoever.

"Who have you helped lately?" I wrote back. "If everyone helped one person anywhere, this world would be a better place. Your comment is truly offensive and ignorant."

I was happy to see a barrage of people I didn't know step up to our defense and give this ignorant guy his comeuppance.

Still, what was most heartbreaking to me was the criticism we received from people we knew. We lost a couple of friends over this drastic change in our life's path. When I started working to bring Teeba here, it never occurred to me that anyone I considered a friend would think I was doing the wrong thing. Apparently I was wrong.

I heard from friends that some of the people in our circle were gossiping behind my back. They thought I was crazy to be doing all of this for Teeba, but they also thought Tim and I were doing it just to get attention.

I wanted to scream at them! Can you imagine your life pivoting a complete 180 degrees at a point when retirement is on the horizon? Can you envision choosing to do something that threatens your job and financial stability, upends your social and family life, and—on top of it all—requires you to spend countless hours in a hospital trying to comfort a little girl screaming in pain and fear? Now, can you envision doing all of that just for attention? Who would do that? It was shocking and hurtful.

As I've reflected on these realities in recent years, I've learned a valuable lesson: the person I was on July 15, 2006, abruptly changed on July 16, 2006.

I think I've changed for the better.

Teeba brought out in me emotions and maturity that I didn't know I had. Before her, I'd spent years only needing to focus on Tim and me and whatever projects came and went in my life. But this wasn't just another project. This innocent little girl from the Sunday newspaper had captured my soul and brought out the maternal instinct I didn't know I still had. A family from the other side of the world, total strangers, had put their trust and faith in me. It was an immense responsibility, and one that I wanted to fulfill with the utmost respect and reverence, especially for Dunia.

I no longer had the patience or desire to allow this kind of hatred or judgment into my life. It was actually freeing. I no longer cared what anyone thought. It's like the old adage that God closes a door but opens a window—we lost people we thought were good friends after Teeba arrived, but it made room for a whole new world of people who have become our friends since then and have made it so much richer.

I thought of the advice I got once from my grandma Sarah, a wonderfully smart and savvy woman whom I often wish had the opportunity to meet Teeba. She wisely told me: "Honey, if someone can't contribute to your life, don't let them take away from it."

CHAPTER 20

TEEBA: SCHOOL DAYS

The average American child sees a police car and feels safe. I felt fear. The average American child doesn't move a muscle at the sight of a tall man heading in their direction. I would flinch. Most American kids play hide-and-seek as a pastime, but when I was little, I played it as an escape from life-threatening situations.

Those were just a few of the ways I was different from the other kids I met after I came to America and started attending school. I can still remember the views and opinions I heard about American kids and their lifestyles when I was in Iraq. Villagers would watch the news, shouting slurs and hateful comments toward the privileges and freedoms of the American people—freedoms they never had the chance to see or experience. I had stepped into this wonderful country under the influence of my grandma, who encouraged me to hate President Bush, hate American culture, and hate the mentality of the US people.

But, as my time in America went by, my eyes were opened. I saw how many people were stepping up to help me—a child from a country the United States was at war with. If the situation was reversed, how many people in my village in Iraq would have stepped up to do the same for an

American child in need? I didn't even know the extent of my blessings at that age, but I could feel the empathy and love surrounding me from all of the people I met over my early months in the United States.

I remember my first day of school vividly. I woke up to my mom Barbara gently scratching my forearms and hands, whispering in her gentle, soothing voice, "Up and at 'em!" She helped me get dressed and ready for school in a green-and-navy plaid dress with my pink raincoat and packed up my pink lunch bag. On that morning, my new backpack actually had to be emptied, not packed, for the first day of school—after we'd bought it a few days earlier I'd been walking around the house packing it full of random objects from the house, like candles or my dad Tim's books.

I was so excited about attending school, but nervous at the same time; I'd never been in a school before. I was also anxious about what the other kids would think about me—not because of my scars, but because I hoped it wasn't obvious that I was wearing a wig. Unfortunately, back then I'd made the choice to be a blond, and with my dark complexion and features, the fact that my hair was a wig was beyond obvious.

After Barbara strapped me into her tan Toyota, we started the three-minute journey to The Goddard School. I remember counting the lines on the road as we drove, which was how I measured how far we'd gone and how much longer before we got there. I gave up after a minute or two because I'd forgotten how to count that high in Arabic.

I'm sure I was like most kids attending school for the first time—I didn't see it as a place created to educate a new generation, just a place where I would be able to play with dolls all day long, which was a dream come true for me. It was just a few minutes away from the house where I was living with Barbara and Tim, but still oceans away from my home.

Not only was attending school a totally unfamiliar experience, but I also did not speak the language well, did not understand the culture, and certainly did not like American food! To me, all American food tasted as if the chef had forgotten to add spices and had only kept the dish on the stove for thirty seconds. In Iraq, we basically burned all our meals to a crispy, crunchy texture, and we added more spices than I can list. I was more familiar with fruit picked directly off the bush, meat that moved from the backyard straight to my plate, and using my fingers to scoop everything into my mouth. Why people did not sit on the ground to eat was beyond my grasp, and silverware was something I previously never knew existed.

More importantly, the English language sounded as if people were whispering and mushing all of their words together, making it hard to know when one sentence ended and the next one started. I thought that all these Americans must have forgotten to roll their tongues to make the "rrrrr" sound, and that the "haggh" sound in the back of their throats must have slipped out of their minds when they spoke. Back at home in Iraq, everyone spoke in a loud, though not harsh, tone. It was not abrasive, just very enunciated.

So as I headed into school for the first time, everything around me felt unfamiliar. The Goddard School was small and snug, with off-white walls and teachers wearing blue smocks. I was greeted by my teacher, Mrs. Robinson, who was a compassionate lady with dark, shiny hair and a wide smile. She showed me the cubby with my name on it where I could put my belongings, then my mom Barbara gave me a few million kisses before leaving. I recall feeling like, *What do I do now?* I felt minuscule, so small in the pond I was now supposed to swim in. I tried my best to think of all the English words I knew.

"Ummm . . . *qahua* . . . umm . . . coffee in *al'iinjlizia*," I chattered to my teacher, meaning coffee is English for *qahua*. She just stared blankly back at me, not understanding.

I had only been there for a few hours before I decided to prance around the crowded room and run into scissors a classmate was holding, cutting my forehead. Neither he nor I realized what had happened until someone pointed it out. It didn't even hurt that much, but of course, five-year-old me had to dramatize the moment.

"Ouch! Ouch! Ouch!" I cried over and over, rubbing my head.

The teacher darted in my direction, her face filled with anxiety and worry.

"Okay? Okay? Are you okay?" she said over and over, along with a bunch of other English words I didn't understand. She said it loud, too, as if I was not only unfamiliar with the language but also hard of hearing.

"Ouch! Ouch! Ouch!" I repeated, mainly because I really didn't know any other English words to say.

It was just me being dramatic, as usual, and soon I was right back to playing with my new friends. I taught the other kids how to say apple in Arabic, while they taught me how to say it in English. At first I was unable to pronounce it with the short *a* sound, so it sounded more like "AHH-pull," until a few hours later when I was finally able to position my mouth the correct way to make the sound. I also remember when lunchtime came around, I asked my teacher repeatedly *"Hal laydayk badhnjan?"* meaning "Do you have an eggplant?"

By the time my mom came to retrieve me from school, I had already cut my head open, taught everyone to say apple in Arabic, and survived a full day of American schooling. So I suppose it was a productive day!

The amazing thing about kids at that age is many of them don't care what you look like. At least not American kids. They were overwhelmingly kind to me, and although I couldn't speak English that clearly, the children would come up and try to talk to me with pointing.

For example, I met a sweet, blond little girl that day who wanted to play with a doll I was holding. To convey this message, she pointed her index finger at her heart, then at mine, then at the doll. I understood she wanted to play with me. The girl was the size of a regular five-year-old, but she was so much taller than me that she made me look like one of the starving, sad African children in TV ads. I had always been a lot smaller than the other kids. The biggest things about me were still my eyes! Regardless of my size and what they might have thought were exotic features and behavior, many of the kids did not even think twice before walking up to me and simply handing me a toy or cookies. Which, by the way, I thought tasted extremely gross.

In my time spent in preschool and kindergarten, I never felt in the classroom that I looked any different. No one said anything to me—and honestly, I don't think anyone cared. One day, my mom came to pick me up from kindergarten, but she arrived early. I wanted to stay and continue to run around, play with Play-Doh, and play dress-up. So my mom sat at the little yellow-and-blue plastic table with me while I molded a hamburger out of blue Play-Doh. I had recently discovered McDonald's, which was one of the only American foods I liked.

As we sat there, I remember whispering to my mom Barbara, pointing to a little girl across the room who was playing with a little toy kitchen and making a plastic meal. It was so noisy that I didn't really need to whisper, but I almost felt embarrassed because the girl I was pointing at was so beautiful. I told my mom I wanted to look like her. She had flawless hands, no scars or redness. Her face did not have a speck on it, and her hair was longer than I had ever seen before. My mom and I talked about how pretty she was, and of course my mom reassured me that I was just as beautiful.

A few minutes later, the girl's mom and little brother walked in to collect her since it was the end of the day. When her mom said it was time to go, the little girl started screaming and hitting her little brother. She rolled her eyes and stomped her feet. Her mom was looking around to make sure no one was watching her daughter's explosive behavior. She was so mean! All her beauty vanished in a few seconds. Her hair was no longer so soft, her face became ugly, and her hands just looked evil.

That day I had my first realization that no matter how beautiful you are, your attitude and intentions are what truly display your beauty. I prayed for that little girl's mother that night because I felt so bad that her daughter had such an ugly manner.

I may not have had any problems with kids at school in those days, but when I went out to any other public place, I would get hundreds of stares. It made me embarrassed in front of my mom Barbara because she was new to this. Every time I went out in America and someone stared at me, I wished my mom Dunia was there because she knew what to do when these things happened in Iraq. She knew that there was nothing she could do to make people stop staring at me, but she always knew how to change my attitude about it. She would stroke her fingers on my face and say I was beautiful, and then remind me that God's opinion of me is all that matters.

I didn't want to burden Barbara with this because it seemed like every time we went out, most of our time was spent either pretending not to see the stares or explaining why my face looked the way it did. Barbara always tried to stand really close to my face, blocking my sight in front and on the sides, so I wouldn't be able to see the kids pointing or staring at me. She tried to protect me all the time, but the stares were nothing new to me. She tried to hide people's reactions from me instead of just talking to me about them. My mom in Iraq did not protect me from everyone, but just said, "Karma will bite them soon," or something similar. When I came to America, Barbara just hid the people from me, but I would still look over her shoulder to see the kids imitating my face or making fun of me. I have always been like this, wanting to know exactly what is going on around me, even when it hurts.

They say ignorance is bliss, but coming from where I grew up, knowledge is an escape. In Iraq, I was always alert and attentive. I always wanted to know exactly what was happening around me—who was nearby, who was walking behind or in front of me, and what I was walking into. I always tried to be prepared because you can't really afford to be surprised in a country like Iraq. I have always been intuitive, so often I can talk to someone for a minute and instantly tell if they have good intentions or bad. My mom Dunia is like this too. She was always able to know who the bad guys were around her, which is why I always felt safe going out with her.

When I was in second grade and had been in the United States about four years, I joined a theatre club at a fine arts institute near my elementary school. That's my first memory of another kid actually speaking directly to me about my scars. We were all second graders, and we were practicing a scene from *The Wizard of Oz*. We had split up into groups of five kids each, and as we were picking out which characters we wanted to be, I said I wanted to be Dorothy.

"You're not pretty enough to be Dorothy," said one of the boys in our group. "Maybe you should be the wicked witch because you look more like her."

I tried to hold back my tears because I did not want him to know it hurt me. I asked to go to the bathroom and washed my hands for a solid five minutes, trying to lessen the appearance of my scars. It didn't work. Without ever telling anyone why, I quit the acting club a week later.

Instances of people hurting me verbally like this have happened so many times over the years. But as I've gotten older, somehow I've found a way to let myself forget about them. When people are rude to me today, I just let it go in one ear and out the other. It's just not worth the storage in my mind. Back then, though, I would hear these things or see someone's reaction and I would immediately try to find a mirror. I became kind of oblivious to my scars, so I would look in the mirror and think, *Why were they so scared? I look fine.* I had just been so used to seeing my face like it was that I couldn't imagine looking different.

135

CHAPTER 21

GROWING DISTANT

Maintaining a connection between Teeba and her mother was becoming more and more difficult the longer she was with us. Often we couldn't get her to talk to her mother at all. She'd complain that she couldn't understand her and couldn't think of anything to say. I knew there were more Arabic words she remembered than she let on, and when I encouraged her to use them she would pretend I was talking gibberish.

"Honey, just say anything. Sing a song, talk about your friends, tell her about school," I would cajole. "Even if she doesn't understand you, she just wants to hear your voice."

And if that didn't work: "Nothing happens until you talk to your mom. No Barbies, no playing outside, no nothing." Sometimes even my threats didn't work, and she would sit silently with her arms crossed during the call. Even though Teeba wanted to stay in the US, Tim and I suspected she still felt hurt deep down that her mother sent her away, and that her insolence during phone calls was her way of expressing it.

Around that time we did find a way to send packages and money to Teeba's family. Shipping things to Iraq was outrageously expensive, and we could never be sure our gifts would make it all the way to them. I was introduced via email to a man named Mohammed "Mo" Khudairi, who runs the Khudairi Group, an engineering and construction company in Iraq. Khudairi Group is headquartered in Houston, Texas, with a regional office in Dubai, in the United Arab Emirates. Mo was born in Iraq but came to the United States with his parents as a child, and his family was filled with such gratitude for their lives in America. When I emailed him and shared our story, he immediately agreed to help.

So we had a new system: I would mail our packages to Houston, and his staff would transport them to the company's Baghdad office. They would hold packages there for Dunia to pick up, or even sometimes deliver them straight to the village. When I wanted to send money, Mo would front it to give to Dunia, and I would pay him back. It was a much safer strategy than what I'd been doing—hiding cash in each package. Mo always made time for me to ask him questions about life in Iraq, and he was so generous with his time and resources. He was a critical point of connection for us with Teeba's family.

Receiving packages and pictures from Teeba helped with Dunia's grief, but I can only imagine how heartbreaking it was for her—not only to be separated from her child during her surgeries but also to watch her slipping away emotionally, refusing to speak to her. And while Dunia and Furat did want Teeba to get the care she needed, they never thought allowing her to come to the United States for medical treatment would mean saying goodbye to her for an entire year. So as we passed the one-year mark of Teeba being in the United States, her family in Iraq became increasingly anxious about the length of time she'd been gone.

They appealed to Steve and Huda for help, asking them to facilitate a reunion with Teeba. It was August 2008, and the insertion of her second set of expanders was scheduled for September. Huda believed strongly that having Teeba see her parents was necessary to sustain her connection to her family, language, religion, and culture. She was increasingly concerned about Teeba's ability to reassimilate when it came time for her to return to Iraq for good. It was part of the Palestine Children's Relief Fund's mission to bring children to the United States for treatment and then return them to their families, so the idea of us keeping her here left Huda and Steve unsettled.

Of course, the thought of Teeba going back to Iraq filled me with anxiety. I loved her with all the fierceness of a mother, and the thought of the danger and violence she would be returning to—and what it would mean for her medical care and education—terrified me. But Tim and I knew we had no right to keep her here against her parents' wishes.

In those days I would often think of the story from 1 Kings 3 when two women came before King Solomon, each of whom had a baby. When one of the babies died, both women claimed the living one was theirs and fought before the king to keep him.

> Then the king said, "Bring me a sword." So they brought a sword for the king. He then gave an order: "Cut the living child in two and give half to one and half to the other."
>
> The woman whose son was alive was deeply moved out of love for her son and said to the king, "Please, my lord, give her the living baby! Don't kill him!"
>
> But the other said, "Neither I nor you shall have him. Cut him in two!"
>
> Then the king gave his ruling: "Give the living baby to the first woman. Do not kill him; she is his mother." (1 Kings 3:24–27)

Although I didn't have a child of my own, I knew Dunia and I would both be like the first mother, willing to give Teeba up to the other if that's what it took to keep her safe and secure.

So we began making plans to reunite her with her family. As I usually do, I started with a grand plan—to bring the entire family here to live in the United States so they could be together but Teeba could continue her surgeries.

Me and my big dreams.

Of course, Huda set me straight immediately. Dunia and Furat had lives, families, and jobs in Iraq, and even securing the visas needed just to bring them here for a visit would be virtually impossible. Plus, it was far outside the bounds of what Steve and Huda could or would help with.

So my Plan B was that I would go to Iraq with Teeba alone, leave her to spend a few months with her family, then come back to get her in the fall so she could resume her surgeries.

"I'm going too," Tim insisted.

"No, you need to stay here," I said. "If Teeba and I get into any trouble, we'll need you here to help get us out. We'll need you to fight for us."

We argued that point for a while, but I felt like I was arguing with a brick wall. "I'm going," Tim repeated. "End of discussion."

Everyone thought we were crazy. People who knew the conditions there warned us that we could be targeted for kidnapping and held for ransom by Al-Qaeda. Or worse, Teeba, her parents, or her siblings could be kidnapped because they had a connection to "wealthy" Americans. Tim and I are tall, and I'm blond and blue eyed, so we would have stuck out like sore thumbs. There would be no blending in.

Thankfully, Steve and Huda once again saved the day with a Plan C—they were willing to let Teeba's family and us stay for a short time in their apartment in Amman, Jordan.

Looming over all of these options, though, was the difficulty we would have getting Teeba back into the United States to continue her treatment. It had taken us a year to get her here to begin with. She had a visitor visa that allowed her to stay in the United States at that time, but if she left, she'd have to start the entire long process of applying for a visa over again, and there were no guarantees she'd ever get the visas she needed to return.

All of these things terrified me, not to mention my fear of traveling to the Middle East during the war. Still, we knew we had to do everything we could to make the reunion happen, so we leapt into action—cancelling Teeba's surgery, checking options for flights, and preparing for the trip. We'd previously scheduled a big family photo shoot in our backyard, right when we were in the midst of this whirlwind of worry and preparation.

While we were struggling to put on happy faces for the photo shoot and hide our worries from Teeba, Huda called. Dunia had abruptly called her to say that she had changed her mind. She said she didn't want Teeba, or us, to take the risk of coming to Iraq, and she believed that Teeba should resume her surgeries. As acute as this crisis was, within twenty-four hours it was over. The news brought us an enormous feeling of relief, but I know it was an enormous devastation for Dunia.

This was how conversations with Teeba's family often went—swinging from crisis to calm in a matter of hours. But after that call, even though the family continued to pressure her, Dunia made sure that I knew her wishes—she wanted Teeba to never return to Iraq. I promised her I would do everything I could to make sure she could stay in the US.

We had no idea how to bridge this gap between our families or what the right choice was. We just made it through day by day, guided only by God.

Teeba's next surgery was rescheduled for September 12, 2008, almost exactly fourteen months after she'd arrived and ten months after Amal had returned to Iraq. This surgery—her seventh—started the entire expansion process over again, inserting new expanders on the right side of her neck and along her left jawline. It would produce enough skin for the first advancement on the right side and the second advancement on the left, using the new skin that had been grafted earlier that year.

Just over a month later, another setback—the surgical incision where the expander had been placed on the left side of her face became partially dehisced, meaning the tissue around the point where the port entered her skin began to break open instead of healing shut and was oozing pus. Surgery number eight repaired the dehisced wound so that Dr. Gosain was able to keep the expander in place and get Teeba through to her second skin graft—surgery number nine—in February 2009. After that surgery she had fresh new skin all the way up to her eyes and forehead on the left side and halfway up her cheek on the right.

Even as Teeba got older and more accustomed to the surgeries, they never got easier for her. Every single one brought with it her same attempts to negotiate and delay, the same begging for me not to do this to her, the same panic when it was time to administer anesthesia, and the same terror as she returned to consciousness. It never got easier for Tim and me, either, seeing this little girl we loved immensely go through long and painful surgeries. We still had all of our same fears and doubts about whether we were doing the right thing—every time.

Still, each time the old burned skin was removed, section by section, and replaced with new fresh skin, it was a reason to celebrate.

Tim, Teeba, and I always talked about how Teeba was one of the lucky ones. Being at Rainbow Babies & Children's Hospital so frequently, we'd seen kids with so many different illnesses and injuries. Many of them could never live the normal life of a child, go to school, spend time with friends, or do the things Teeba got to do—go swimming, take dance classes, or play sports. Some of them never got to go home to their families at all.

Eventually, Teeba got to see others like her who had experienced severe burns. She was invited to attend a special camp for children who had been burned, and at "burn camp," as she called it, she met other children who had been injured to a far worse degree than she had. One child was burned when her parents, high on drugs, locked her in a closet and set her on fire, believing the bow on her dress was the Devil. Another was put in a scalding bathtub by her mother. And another was burned when someone threw a homemade bomb through the window of their house—she survived, but her grandmother and siblings died. One of these children had nothing but stumps for hands—all ten fingers had been scorched off. With that level of injury, the kind of reconstructive surgery Teeba was getting wasn't even an option.

It was during one of Teeba's surgeries that our dear friend Huda was in the same hospital, battling leukemia. We met her in the cafeteria, both she and Teeba sitting in wheelchairs talking. Teeba had always admired Huda's hair—thick, dark, and hanging past her shoulders. But now, due to her chemotherapy, Huda's hair was thin and brittle and beginning to fall out. It was surreal to see them sitting together, their partially bald heads exposed, the life draining from Huda's body as Teeba's was being made whole.

Sadly, Huda died on July 15, 2009, at the age of forty-six. Without Huda and Steve, Teeba might never have had the opportunity to come to the United States to receive treatment. They devoted so much love and energy for Teeba's sake, epitomizing Jesus' words: "Greater love has no one than this: to lay down one's life for one's friends" (John 15:13).

I'll be forever grateful to them.

CHAPTER 22

TEEBA: MISSING HOME

I loved and missed my family in Iraq like crazy. But my way of dealing with these feelings was to simply pretend to hate them all. I missed my mom Dunia and my dad Furat, and I yearned to see them again. But I kept my distance and would act up anytime I was told to speak to them on the phone. I felt betrayed—like I was a burden to them—and I believed that's why they shipped me halfway across the world. At that age, I didn't know giving up a child is the hardest thing a mother could do. I just figured my family got bored of me or something.

Not speaking to them, however, was a big reason why I forgot my Arabic and let so many memories slip out of my mind. When I did speak to my mom on those rare occasions, I told her how mad I was at my grandma for leaving me in America. I told her it wasn't fair to make me come back to Iraq, not because I didn't want to go, but because I didn't want her to think I still loved her. Which I did. I wanted to stay in America, but I also wanted to have my family come over and live with me.

Being in America was amazing, but many times I hated not being around my family and Iraq's exotic culture, beautiful music, loud voices, delicious spicy foods, and—most of all—the desert. I missed it all horribly, and when my grandma left, I really had no one to talk to, no one who understood my past.

That's the thing about surviving something extreme, like a bombing in my case. Everyone wants you to tell them your story and asks how you've been so strong through it all, as if I had an answer. I never knew what to say. There's no secret formula to surviving something that should have killed you. There's no easy way to be a child in a country oceans away from your family. There's no shortcut to easing the physical pain of an explosion.

Because no one knew how I felt, no one understood that it was the small things I missed—hugs from my parents, Iraqi food, and the dust flying in the air during the Maghrib prayer, which is said at sunset. I remember my uncle sweeping the perimeter of our house, and the wind would whip the sand around in the air as the sun set. My dad would tell my sister and me to stay in the house until my uncle was done sweeping so we wouldn't get sand in our eyes. I missed sitting on the roof holding my dad's hand. I missed waking up to the smell of potatoes burning to a crisp.

I didn't talk about these thoughts with anyone except my mom Barbara. There was always a battle between saying what was on my mind and not wanting to hurt those who had given me everything they could. I thought, *If I admit I miss my dad Furat, will my dad Tim be offended? If I share that I like Arabic food more than American food, will my mom Barbara be hurt?* I didn't want to offend anyone, and I didn't want to hear people sympathize and try to compare my life experiences to a little cut they got when they were four.

So, those were the thoughts I had when people asked me questions about my story or about Iraq. Back then I would just nod along and tell people what they wanted to hear: "I love America" or "I am happier here." That was all true, but I didn't want to go further into explaining my conflicting feelings to people I knew couldn't understand.

For the most part, I kept these thoughts to myself.

CHAPTER 23

THE ODDS ARE
AGAINST US

On a frigid afternoon in January 2010, a FedEx envelope was waiting for me on the front porch when I arrived home from picking Teeba up from her after-school Daisy Scouts meeting. It had been snowing, and I plucked the package off our snow-dusted porch and brought it inside, still shaking the flurries off my coat and stomping snow from my boots. A typical first grader, Teeba bounced out of the car and ran inside, loaded down by her pink princess backpack and holding an art project she and the other Daisies had just completed.

I dumped my briefcase and purse on the table, then stood and stared at the envelope for a few moments. A knot formed in my stomach. The sender was the Office of US Citizenship and Immigration Services (USCIS), part of the Department of Homeland Security. I knew exactly what was inside, but I couldn't be sure if it brought good news or bad.

By this point we'd already managed to get four renewals of Teeba's visa from USCIS. When Teeba came to the United States, she was admitted under a B-2 visa, which is also known as a tourist visa. It's hard to imagine major reconstructive surgery fitting into the same category as a Colorado ski vacation or a week on the beach in Key West, but according to the US government, the criteria are the same—she could only stay for a limited period of time, and it had to be clear to the US government that she intended to return to her home country and had financial resources to support her while she was here. Each visa was valid for six months.

When her first visa expiration came up in February 2008, shortly before her first skin graft, I was a nervous wreck. We got Dr. Gosain to write a letter to USCIS laying out Teeba's treatment plan, explaining that it would require her to stay in the United States at least throughout the remainder of 2008 and 2009.

Given that and her age, those four renewals went through smoothly. But with my lack of knowledge about the immigration system, each of those renewals seemed scary and uncertain. Every time I mailed off one of those renewal applications and a $400 check to Homeland Security, the possibility that Teeba could lose her legal status and be deported loomed over our heads. Even though I had a document signed by her parents giving me power of attorney in September 2008, that didn't mean that I had any legal standing to keep her here if the US government denied her visa renewal requests.

Tim and I were told over and over that the odds were against us in keeping her here. Eventually our time with her would run out, and we could never be sure when that might happen.

But as I stood looking at the envelope on that cold January morning, the possibility of Teeba returning to Iraq for good seemed unthinkable for us.

By now, Teeba was eight and had lived in the United States for three and a half years. She was completely Americanized, spoke no Arabic, was attending school, and still going through constant medical treatments. With each setback in the expansion process, the timeline for her treatment plan had become longer and longer.

Returning Teeba to Iraq would have been like dropping any other eight-year-old American girl in the middle of one of the most dangerous countries on earth. Violence there had only increased, not lessened. She would have faced all of the same dangers we worried about back when we considered taking her home in 2008, like kidnapping for ransom. It was highly unlikely that she would be able to continue her education, and she wouldn't be able to get the kind of medical care she needed to continue her reconstructive surgery. Plus, Amal was still insisting that Teeba marry her cousin when she turned twelve. Considering her appearance and their village's culture, it would have been difficult for the family to find a husband for her, and she might never live independently.

But another dilemma arose as Teeba was nearing the end of kindergarten at The Goddard School. Anyone from a foreign country who is in the United States with a B-2 visa cannot attend school, even if they'd come here for medical treatment and even if they're a child.

The only way for Teeba to attend school in the United States was to have F-1 status, which is the same kind of visa that international students get when they come to America to study. But she couldn't attend public school, and her other choices were limited—it had to be a school approved by the Department of Homeland Security. If her medical treatment at some point prevented her from keeping her full-time student status, or if she didn't keep up her grades, she could lose her student visa and be deported. Same thing if she got into any trouble, which obviously wasn't a concern in first grade but could be later on. If she ever left the United States, her whole case would be reopened and we'd have to start all over applying for an F-1 visa, which could take months. The whole thing made my head spin.

There were other issues at play as well. Financially, Tim and I had been comfortable before Teeba arrived, but back then we were two empty nesters close to retirement. Right before Teeba arrived, we'd decided to make some real estate investments in Naples, Florida, hoping to continue to fund our retirement by renting to snowbirds and vacationers. When the 2008 housing crisis hit, it devastated the Florida real estate market; our investments crumbled. Tim's residential cleaning business hit hard times, too, as his customers cut back on unnecessary expenses.

As all this was happening, we were simultaneously taking on more and more responsibility in caring for a child with complex medical needs. Even though Dr. Gosain and University Hospitals were providing Teeba's reconstructive surgery free of charge, Tim and I still assumed all of her additional medical costs. Because we were not her legal guardians at that time, we couldn't put her on our insurance. We paid for every checkup and prescription out of pocket. Plus, we were sending Dunia money and paying hundreds of dollars a month on international phone calls.

As Teeba prepared to enter first grade, we were fortunate enough to find a private school that was close to our house and met the Department of Homeland Security criteria. But it was expensive—about $13,000 for first grade alone.

Despite all of these stresses, we applied for Teeba to receive F-1 status and enrolled her in school for first grade in the fall of 2009. She started school, made new friends, joined Daisy Scouts, and fell in love with her first-grade teachers—all of this even as Tim and I knew, with dread in our guts, that the F-1 status wasn't a sure bet.

All of this was on my shoulders as I grabbed the tab at the end of that FedEx envelope and pulled. I remember the ripping sound it made. This was the moment we would find out the fate of Teeba's education and her future in the United States.

As I reached inside, I found just a single sheet of paper:

> This courtesy notice is to advise you to action taken on this case. The official notice has been mailed to the attorney or representative indicated above. Any relevant documentation included in the notice was also mailed . . .

Blah, blah, blah. I kept scanning until I saw it:

> The above application for change of nonimmigrant status is *approved*.

Teeba could stay in the US! She could stay in school! Once again, God had cleared our path against all odds.

⊸⊱

Tim and I tried our best to keep all these uncertainties from Teeba. She never knew about everything going on behind the scenes to keep her in the United States. We wanted her to live the life of a normal American child as much as possible amidst all of the expanders and surgeries. We worried that her childhood was slipping away, replaced by surgeries, having to be a "big girl," enduring people's stares, being separated from her family, and trying to fit in.

So in February 2010, my friend Paula and I decided to take advantage of a break between surgeries to take eight-year-old Teeba and Paula's son Jackson to Walt Disney World. Teeba had been here nearly three years by that point, had received her second skin graft, and would soon have her third set of expanders inserted. We explored the park, rode the rides, saw the shows, bought mindless trinkets, and ate whatever goodies we felt like. When we visited Mickey and Minnie's House for the "meet and greet" with the characters, we made sure to be the last ones in line for pictures, so that Mickey and Minnie were able to spend a little extra time and attention on Teeba and Jackson.

But I knew exactly the destination that would make Teeba's day. At eight years old, she still loved the Disney princesses, so we headed to Cinderella Castle to have lunch, shop, and visit the Bibbidi Bobbidi Boutique—a beauty salon that transforms girls into their favorite princesses with a new hairstyle, makeup, princess gown, and more.

I was holding Teeba as we walked up to the front desk to see if I could get her on the schedule, only to find out appointments had to be made many weeks in advance. I was more disappointed than she was—she didn't really realize what was happening, but I always wanted her to have special experiences to offset the discomfort of her surgeries. I tried to take it in stride, and we headed out of the castle to our next adventure.

"Excuse me, ma'am?" I turned to see one of the women from the boutique running after me.

Looking at Teeba's face, she said, "We'd really like to make this happen for your daughter. We have a pretty packed schedule, but if you can be patient we can fit her in today."

As we followed her back into the salon, Teeba's eyes lit up when she saw a room that was worthy of being on a movie set, filled with princess costumes, shoes, wigs, and accessories. After much deliberation, she chose to be transformed into the princess Belle from *Beauty and the Beast*. The layers upon layers of yellow fabric and lace dwarfed her tiny body, and her yellow slip-on princess shoes flopped when she walked. Over her own wig, the stylists put on a Belle wig of long dark hair with tendrils falling around her face.

By then she'd been through two rounds of expanders, with fresh, smooth skin on her forehead and most of both cheeks. It was still a jigsaw of fresh and scarred skin, but after ten surgeries the smooth skin was finally winning out over the burned skin.

There were three women fussing all around her at this time—one styling her hair, one doing makeup, and one polishing her nails. It was clear that on this day, Teeba felt like the most beautiful little girl on the planet. Her smile couldn't get any bigger, and her eyes sparkled like stars. I sat watching and crying—tears of happiness for Teeba.

Then Teeba destroyed my reverie by insisting that the stylists target me next. As much as I objected, they dragged me into one of their chairs, outfitted me with a crazy Sleeping Beauty wig, and attempted to apply princess makeup over my eyes, which were swollen and red from crying. They did the best they could, but I felt like some kind of dragon.

Not Teeba. She thought that I, too, was a beautiful princess.

We stepped back out into the park, me trying to hide my garish face, but Teeba striding with her head up and full of confidence. The day's surprises weren't over, though—when we went back into Mickey's House, all of the princesses and Prince Charming were waiting for Teeba to have their pictures taken with her. She was floating on air, with her head held high and her eyes transfixed on these characters. After she'd collected all of their signatures in her autograph book and had her picture taken with each one, we headed to the front desk to pay, our faces hurting from so much smiling and me still drying my tears. I got out my wallet, but the cashier waved a hand at me. The park had picked up the entire tab.

This was just one of many, many instances when people took the time and interest to do acts of great kindness for Teeba. All the pain of her surgeries and fears of the unknown were always balanced by people reaching out from the goodness of their hearts. The world and the people in it are noble.

While Teeba's external appearance was not optimal as she went through years of expanders and skin grafts, she made up for it in her outsized personality. Some children in her situation might have taken all the stares, taunts, pain, and struggles, and turned them inward, becoming withdrawn and fearful.

Teeba did the opposite.

Everywhere we went, people were drawn to Teeba. She demonstrated a maturity far beyond her years, with a sharp wit and a constant desire to try new things. She was always performing—dressing up for elaborate Hannah Montana concerts, choreographing dances with her friends, or starring in her own cooking show as her made-up character Rose BeGoes. She relished the opportunity to go for a manicure and pedicure with Maria. She loved clothes but never dressed up as a way of minimizing her appearance or hiding her scars. She accepted herself as she was and usually acted as if there was nothing at all different about her.

Teeba's life experiences taught her early on to be persistent. She was a master negotiator, working tirelessly to wear us down when she really wanted something. She was the ringleader in her friend groups, and she didn't always get the concept of compromise. She rarely shied away from new experiences or people, unless they did something to insult or hurt her. Even then, she would hold those feelings close to the vest, often not sharing those hurtful incidents with me for weeks. As outgoing as she was, she was not outwardly affectionate with anyone but Tim and me, and she was always guarded with her true emotions.

As Teeba grew older, she developed an innate ability to understand other people, including their intentions and their needs. In her grew a gift for using her experiences to benefit others, especially other kids who had experienced the kinds of tragedies she had.

In 2012, I met with Dr. Gosain and Sharon Klonowski, director of the Rainbow Babies & Children's Hospital Circle of Friends, which recruits groups of donors and volunteers to support the hospital's foundation. I offered to start a support group called Circle of Families for others going through the same grueling plastic-surgery process with their children. I teamed up with Meredith Farrow, whose daughter Presley was going through reconstructive surgery with Dr. Gosain for a cleft lip and palate, to create a fund-raising event called Save a Smile, Save a Child.

Our first Save a Smile, Save a Child event in 2012 drew more than four hundred people, including local sports and media celebrities. Across the stage were large photos of the amazing transformations of Dr. Gosain's patients, including Teeba and Presley. Those images spoke volumes about the work that Dr. Gosain and his team did every day.

Teeba was one of the featured speakers. She'd been in the US for five years and was between her second and third rounds of expansion. She was ten but still tiny for her age, so when it was her turn to speak she grabbed a milk crate she found backstage and dragged it over to the podium. As people saw this little girl, all dressed up in a little blue dress with white polka dots and white leggings, pulling a milk crate, they immediately gave her all their attention. She'd curled her hair and put on the tiniest amount of lip gloss, and she exuded confidence, smiling out over the crowd. I could see immediately that my help was not needed, so I slipped away to one side.

Teeba made an exaggerated *tap, tap, tap* on the microphone. "Can I have everyone's attention please?"

You could have heard a pin drop. The room went absolutely silent.

"Hello, my name is Teeba Furat Marlowe," she began. She thanked everyone for being there, then looked down at her speech. "I just want to say thank you for helping children in this wonderful hospital. I am a patient there and I have wonderful news. The doctors there are sooo amazing. You have changed my life. Now, without further ado, I would like to read you something I wrote":

Life will reward you if you just do the right thing, even the hard and painful. It is amazing how people can be so mean. Even if you do something very nice, you can get your heart broken.

Because I am going through some tough times with all my surgeries and expanders, sometimes I feel left out because some people get afraid of me. Sometimes they are not afraid but curious, so I try to tell them but they just do not understand. So they grow to be afraid of me. Sometimes I get real mad, but it is okay because I know the people I know love me with all their hearts.

Love is the answer, and people that care about you will really show it. Just look into that person's eyes and you will know.

"And that was it, so enjoy the rest of your night. Umm . . . see you. I guess."

There was a moment of complete silence. Then the crowd burst into deafening applause and everyone rose to their feet. It wasn't the type of polite applause you might hear after a normal speech. It was a rousing show of approval and acceptance. She and her friends then got to hand over one of those huge cardboard checks to Dr. Gosain to honor the sizeable donation made by the law firm I work for, Dworken & Bernstein.

Afterward, people came up to me in tears, gushing about her poise, her presence, and her words. Others showered Teeba with congratulations and praise. But by then she'd gone back to being just a regular old kid again—running around with her friends and sneaking away with any microphones she could find so they could "perform."

This was Teeba.

CHAPTER 24

HOME TO STAY

Okay, it's time to call Mama Dunia!" I chirped as the three of us gathered around the speakerphone in the kitchen, along with Leila, who was there to help us with translation. Teeba hopped up on the counter next to me as I dialed the long string of numbers to make the international call to Iraq.

"You need to tell Mama Dunia all about school and sledding!" I said to Teeba as we listened to the phone ring and ring. Then, we heard those three familiar beeps to indicate a failed call. We tried again. This time it was just dead air for several seconds, then those same three beeps.

"Ugh, this is so frustrating," I sighed as we tried another of the three numbers we had for their home and cell phones. Same thing again—dead air, failed call.

Finally, on the third try, the phone crackled to life.

"*Alo!*" I smiled to hear Dunia's sweet voice, and we all called out "Hello!" in English.

Leila and Dunia greeted each other, then gave nine-year-old Teeba a chance to talk to her mother. It was 2011 and she had been in the US nearly five years. She'd forgotten all of her Arabic, but there were a few

Arabic phrases that Leila would prod her to use. Otherwise we had to rely completely on Leila's translations.

"I love you, Mama!" Teeba called out.

"I love you!" Dunia responded in English. It was one of the only English phrases she knew.

"Teeba, say *schlonich*," Leila whispered to her.

"*Schlonich!*" Teeba shouted, meaning "How are you?"

"Teeba, sing a song for Mama Dunia," I urged, and she began singing a song she'd made up about flowers.

"That is beautiful!" Dunia said. I could hear the smile in her voice hearing her daughter sing.

Leila and Dunia then launched into a long and loud conversation in Arabic. These were the most frustrating parts of our conversations with Teeba's family. Sometimes Leila and Dunia would go back and forth for ten minutes, and we were left wondering what they were saying while Teeba would get bored and beg to go play.

On this day, we were sitting and waiting while Leila and Dunia continued their conversation in Arabic. We tried our best to be patient waiting for a translation, but sometimes our patience wore out.

"Leila, what is she saying?" Tim butted in after several minutes, clearly irritated. She held up a finger and kept talking.

But gradually we realized that something was wrong. Dunia's voice caught, and it sounded like she was struggling not to cry.

"Leila, what is it? What's wrong?" I said again.

She got Dunia to pause for a minute, then told us: "Dunia and Furat want Teeba to stay for her surgeries. But she says that people in the village are saying, 'How could you leave your daughter?' They are saying that Teeba should come back," Leila told us. "Since people in the village are talking, Amal says she is going to come here and take Teeba back to Iraq, and they had a huge argument about it."

Slowly, a cloud gathered on Teeba's face as she realized what Leila was saying. Leila returned to her conversation with Dunia, and Teeba brought her eyes to meet mine.

"I don't want to go back," she whispered, as tears welled up in her eyes and she reached for me. "I want to stay in America. I don't want anyone to come and take me."

Leila managed to get Dunia to pause again for a minute, then turned to us. "Amal is telling Dunia that she can't come here because she is too young, and that Amal has to be the one to come get Teeba," Leila said.

By now Teeba was sobbing.

"No! I want to stay in America!" she shouted in the direction of the speakerphone. And then to me: "Mommy, I don't want to go anyplace. I want to stay here!"

"Honey, your mom and dad want you to stay for your surgeries," Leila told her, trying to comfort her. "You don't need to worry. Your grandma can't come back and get you."

Leila returned to her conversation with Dunia while Teeba sobbed into my shoulder. Tim stood beside us, rubbing her back.

"I promise you, you're not going anywhere," I murmured, my cheek against hers. "Dad and I aren't going to allow it."

"This isn't fair!" Teeba wailed. "I hate Iraq! What is there to like about it? Nothing is good there!"

"There are only four people who can say anything about what you do," Tim told her softly, "your mom and dad and Mom and me. That's it. We're going to do everything that we can to keep you here."

This wasn't the first or last time we heard about this tension in Teeba's family. Amal wanted Teeba home so she could marry her cousin when she became a teenager. Dunia was bearing the brunt of criticism from Amal, while others in her village were hurling insults at her too. All the abuse was taking its toll on Dunia.

Amazingly, Dunia continued to stand firm in her insistence that Teeba never return to Iraq, despite the pressure from her in-laws and neighbors. Dunia knew, now more than ever, that there would never be a way for Teeba to live safely there.

It wasn't until April 2013 that people in the United States began hearing the term *ISIS*, but long before that, the foundations were being laid for this vicious terrorist group. Sadly, their extremist mission was bringing ever-increasing violence to Teeba's hometown in Diyala Province. It seemed that every day we heard more terrifying news out of Iraq, all of which increased our feeling of urgency to find a way for Teeba to stay in the United States.

Tim and I always dreamed of finding a way for Teeba and Dunia to see each other again. The problem was that leaving the country with an F-1 student visa would make the process of returning to the United States long and complicated.

Tim and I had been appointed Teeba's legal guardians in 2010, but that had no impact on her ability to stay in the country. The only way to be sure she could remain here, and yet pave the way for her to be able to eventually visit her family, was to pursue legal residency, which would give her a green card and many of the same protections that an American citizen has. Then when she turned eighteen, she could apply to become a naturalized US citizen.

We talked through our plan with Dunia, she agreed, and we started laying the groundwork for a green card application. But getting Teeba a green card wouldn't be quick or easy. Our immigration attorney, Kim Alabasi, found a strategy that wasn't well known at the time—Special Juvenile Immigrant Status. It's only available to children who are already in this country and have a legal guardian. Kim had to make a case in court that reunification between Teeba and her family would be impossible—though through no fault of their own—and that returning her to her home country would not be in her best interests. But even if the court found in our favor, that would only give us the *opportunity* to apply for a green card with the Department of Homeland Security.

There were no guarantees.

We *had* to make this work. Kim, Tim, and I built up a mountain of supporting documents—including letters from Dr. Gosain and a wide variety of people who knew us. This was one of the times the media coverage Teeba had received was helpful; we had many people who knew her story and were willing to step up on her behalf. Kim's husband, Hayder, an Iraqi who came to this country as a refugee in 1992 and returns there frequently, wrote an affidavit describing firsthand the dangers of life in Diyala Province, the threat of potential kidnapping Teeba could face if she returned, and the lack of access to education and medical care there. All three of us were evaluated by a psychologist, and Kim assembled a research report on the climate in Iraq and Teeba's family's circumstances in fine detail.

But the best spokesperson was Teeba herself. In a letter to the court, she explained her case this way:

> I'm going to tell you why I would love to stay in America. First let me tell you there is nothing I love more than my parents here and in Iraq. I would love to visit my real parents, but not yet, at least not until I am 30 or maybe late 20s.
>
> I love both my families equal. I don't want to go to Iraq because it's not safe there and I could never let go of this life. I feel God gave me this new life because of what happened in Iraq. I think He is giving me a second chance. I feel so safe here and loved. I don't ever want to leave. I hope you understand.
>
> I am learning so much, there are so many people who love and care for me. I have great friends that I love very much. Even my dance teacher loves me, and I don't think I could do all of this in Iraq.
>
> I love America. :-)
>
> Love, Teeba Furat Marlowe

We filed the paperwork with our county probate court on March 1, 2013. Then we began to pray.

We got our first glimmer of hope almost immediately—our case was assigned to the docket of Judge Ted Klammer, the same judge who had granted our legal guardianship. Judge Klammer knew us and Teeba's story, and he understood our intentions.

But before the case even reached his desk, Judge Klammer died suddenly. He was a well-loved part of our community, and his sudden death was tragic. But it also brought a fresh wave of worries for our case. Applications for Special Juvenile Immigrant Status weren't common at that time, so many judges had never seen a case like this. When a retired judge from another part of the state was assigned to take over Judge Klammer's cases, we had no idea what he would think of our request, not knowing anything about us or our story.

Kim requested a meeting with the new judge. She took with her all of our supporting materials and described Teeba's circumstances—her injuries in Iraq, our efforts to bring her here and care for her, the surgeries she'd already endured, and the medical and educational needs she'll have in the future. The judge agreed, and we got our first small victory—on April 25, 2013, the court found in favor of Teeba's Special Juvenile Immigrant Status, clearing the way for us to apply to USCIS for her green card. We said a prayer, Kim filed the application, and we settled in for what we knew could be a long wait.

Throughout the summer of 2013, I logged onto the USCIS website twice every day to see if they'd made a decision on her green card—every morning when I reached my office, and every afternoon before I headed home.

Pending.

Pending.

Pending.

Every day, the same thing. For months.

On Friday, September 6, checking my afternoon email one last time before heading home for the weekend, I found this automatically generated email, the kind of message the average person might have deleted if they hadn't been watching and waiting for it for four months like I had:

From: USCIS

To: Barbara Marlowe

Application Type: I485, APPLICATION TO REGISTER PERMANENT RESIDENCE OR TO ADJUST STATUS

Your Case Status: Card/Document Production

On September 6, 2013, we ordered production of your new card. Please allow 30 days for your card to be mailed to you. If we need something from you we will contact you. If you move before you receive the card, call customer service at 1–800–375–5283.

Please do not respond to this email message.

Sincerely,

The U.S. Citizenship and Immigration Services (USCIS)

Teeba had been approved for a green card! I couldn't scream out loud at work, but I was screaming inside: *Teeba is now a legal permanent resident!*

Relief and joy flooded through my body, and tears leapt to my eyes. I dialed Tim at home.

"Honey! Honey! She got approved! Teeba got approved for her green card!" I cried into the phone, trying to stay quiet and not make a total scene in my office.

"Oh, what a relief!" Tim said. "I was so worried."

But a single automatically generated email still wasn't enough to set my anxious heart at ease. I wouldn't rest easy until I was holding that little green piece of plastic in my hands. So it became a new ritual—instead of checking the USCIS portal twice daily, I would check the mailbox daily, as soon as I got home from work, as those thirty days counted down.

Finally, one day, there it was.

I clutched the envelope to my chest and ran into the house. I wanted to open it with Tim and Teeba there for a grand unveiling.

I ripped open the envelope and whipped out the package inside ceremoniously. "Honey, guess what this is! You now have a green card!" Tim and I were crying, but at ten years old, Teeba didn't quite get it. She kind of shrugged her shoulders.

"Honey, do you realize how many people would *love* to have a green card?" I said. "Do you realize how important this is to your future?"

It was "honey this" and "honey that"—to her, I probably looked like a crazy person ranting about a green piece of plastic. She just looked at me and gave me that eye roll. Tim was still elated, but he also started laughing as he saw this moment unfold.

This was the culmination of six years of worry, anxiety, and sleepless nights—the constant fear that I could lose my Teeba to some government bureaucracy. As long as she stayed out of trouble, she would always have the ability to stay in the United States, no matter where life took her. I'd had daily conversations with God, asking Him to clear a path that would allow Teeba to stay in America where she could be safe, pursue her education, and get the treatment she needs.

God answered those prayers—Teeba was now a legal permanent resident.

But what I didn't realize was that even with a green card, Teeba still needed her Iraqi passport to leave the country. I discovered that fact when we tried to take a vacation with our family friends to Mexico, and we showed up at the airport with only Teeba's green card. We were able to scramble my brother-in-law Rick and sister-in-law Noreen out to our house at 5:00 a.m. to grab her passport and race it to us at the airport, which rescued a family vacation we'd hoped to take with Teeba for seven years but couldn't because of expanders, surgeries, school, and visa challenges.

The trip was saved, but I noticed Teeba's Iraqi passport was just six months from expiring. That could be a problem.

I started calling the Iraqi Consulate in Detroit to begin the process of renewing her passport, only to have voicemail after voicemail unreturned. After weeks of trying, I turned to the Iraqi Embassy in Washington DC, who directed me back to the Consulate in Detroit. Again, no response. We already knew it usually took two or three visits to the Consulate to complete all of the steps in an Iraqi passport renewal, and time was ticking. If Teeba's passport expired, it would be extremely difficult to get all of the necessary paperwork we would need from her parents in Iraq to get a new passport. Getting a US passport was not an option. But with no valid passport, she could never leave the country.

As a last-ditch effort, I reached out to a man named Omar Humadi, an American-born Iraqi whom I'd met several years prior through a mutual friend. Omar had been working in the Ohio government back then, so I hoped he might have some advice for me.

"Iraq has a million problems," Omar laughed. "They are understaffed and overwhelmed."

"Do you know anyone there?" I asked. "Do you have any advice for us?"

"Well, Barbara, I don't live in Ohio anymore . . ." he began, and I sighed, assuming he'd left government service. I'd have to go back to trying to figure this out for myself.

"Now I live in New York," Omar continued. "I'm the special assistant to Mohamed Ali Alhakim, the Iraqi ambassador to the United Nations."

I just about fell out of my chair. I'd called Omar on a whim, only to realize I now had a direct line to the Iraqi ambassador himself. (In the years since, Mohamed Ali Alhakim has continued to rise in Iraqi politics. He is now the Foreign Minister of Iraq.)

Immediately, Omar briefed Ambassador Ali Alhakim on our situation, and the ambassador personally contacted the Iraqi Consulate in Detroit to instruct them to initiate our paperwork. I received a call from the Consulate within hours, and they not only informed me they had begun initiating Teeba's paperwork, but they also offered to send a car to Cleveland, more than two hundred miles away, to bring us to the Consulate for Teeba to be fingerprinted.

I'm someone who prefers to control my surroundings, so I politely declined the offer of a private car. But when we arrived, it was as if they'd rolled out the red carpet just for thirteen-year-old Teeba. The Consulate General insisted on meeting Teeba personally, presented her with a Miss Kitty watch and a pin in the shape of Iraq, and spent about forty-five minutes visiting with us.

There were still obstacles, though. Right after Teeba's fingerprints were transmitted to Baghdad for her passport renewal, the entire computer system there was locked down after an ISIS attack. Miraculously, Teeba's application just made it through, and her passport arrived a couple of months later via diplomatic pouch, saving us a trip to Detroit to pick it up.

Not long after that, Omar called to say that Ambassador Alhakim wanted to meet Teeba. He invited us to visit the United Nations in New York. Just a few weeks later, Teeba, Tim, and I watched, amazed, as Omar whisked us past the long lines of tourists and gave us our own personal tour of the United Nations. We even got to observe part of a meeting of the Middle East ambassadors, who we learned later were discussing the rise of ISIS and its practice of harvesting human body parts. At the end of the tour, I expected Teeba, Tim, and I would have a brief meet-and-greet with the ambassador at the United Nations before being sent on our way.

I was wrong.

Instead, Omar told us that Ambassador Alhakim wanted us to visit him at the embassy—called The Permanent Mission of the Republic of Iraq—for a longer visit. It was quite an honor—we were only expecting a few minutes with him on our way out of the United Nations building. The building was a towering beige brick brownstone guarded by a tall iron gate, marked with a gold etched sign that read "The Permanent Delegation of Iraq to the United Nations."

It was a bitter cold but sunny February day, and the bold red, white, and black bars of the Iraqi flag—marked with the Arabic words *Allāhu akbar* ("God is great") in green—waved against the blue sky. Omar navigated us past security and momentarily waited with us outside Ambassador Alhakim's private reception room before we were shown in by an assistant.

As we waited for the ambassador to join us, we gazed around the elegant room with rich wood floors framing intricately designed rugs and heavy floor-to-ceiling drapes. Photos of Iraq's previous UN ambassadors graced the walls, along with an Iraqi flag and the blue UN flag, which bore the familiar logo of the world map surrounded by two olive branches.

Soon, the ambassador appeared, wearing a broad smile.

"Barbara, Tim, Teeba, this is Ambassador Alhakim," said Omar.

The ambassador entered the room with a smile. He was short in stature but tall in grace and kindness. He warmly grasped each of our hands and hugged Teeba, while his assistants brought in tea.

"As soon as Omar told me your story, Teeba, I knew I had to meet you," he said. "It is so nice to finally meet you and I'm very glad I was able to help you with your passport issue."

He listened attentively to Teeba's answers as he peppered her with questions.

"Teeba, tell me, what do you think of America? What do you like about school?"

She was uncharacteristically shy, clearly a little intimidated by the circumstances.

Ambassador Alhakim shared stories of his family, and Teeba showed him pictures of hers, while we sipped tea out of delicate china cups. He and Omar made us feel like they had nothing else to do but spend the afternoon with us.

Then he called for his assistant, and he entered the room with an armful of special gifts for us. For Teeba he had an iPad Mini, a framed display of Iraqi currency, a gold plate with the ancient symbol of Iraq—an Assyrian human-headed winged bull (*lamassu*)—and a small gold camel figurine with a jewel-encrusted saddle on his hump. The hump lifted up to reveal a small space to store a ring or necklace. He presented Tim with a long jewelry box containing delicate Islamic prayer beads made of glass, usually called *misbaha* or *tesbih*.

We spent nearly an hour with Ambassador Alhakim. As we prepared to say goodbye, he turned to Teeba.

"Teeba, when you turn eighteen, I would like to offer you an internship at the UN," he said. She broke into a big smile, envisioning how cool it would be to live and work in New York City someday. Before we said goodbye, he asked about her upcoming surgeries; when she had the next one, the ambassador sent a beautiful arrangement of flowers to our home.

I couldn't believe the journey we'd just experienced: all the way from my frustration with an expiring passport to a personal visit with the Iraqi Ambassador to the UN. Yet these are the types of journeys on which Teeba has constantly taken us over the years. Somehow, everything always works out when it comes to Teeba.

CHAPTER 25

A CONNECTION
BETWEEN MOTHERS

By 2014, I had been caring for another woman's child for seven years, and I still didn't feel I really knew Teeba's mother. Even though we had loving friends willing to freely give of their time to translate our calls with Dunia, I still acutely felt the distance between us, and my heart ached to close it.

Plus, our phone bills were reaching hundreds of dollars every month with calls to Iraq, and the reliability of the connection had only gotten worse. Sometimes we'd try calling her for hours only to hear a message in Arabic stating the line was unavailable—either due to cell towers being damaged in fighting or spotty access to electricity to charge their phones. We tried to Skype, but that could only be done when a relative was able to make the connection on their end, and most of the time the clarity was gray and fuzzy.

When I did manage to reach Dunia, I certainly didn't want to cut it short, so the conversations we did have were long and expensive. As Teeba had gotten older, her attitude toward calling her family had improved somewhat, but her conversations were flat and emotionless. With every call, she would just repeat the same phrases over and over:

"How are you?"

"I love you!"

"I am thinking of you!"

"How is Fatima?"

"How is Maryam?"

"How is Aboody?"

At the time we were getting help with translations from an Iraqi woman living in Cleveland named Nazek Al-Malak, who was always quick to help any Iraqis who moved here or came to our area for medical treatment. She was one of those who had visited Amal and Teeba back when they were at the Ronald McDonald House and had even invited them to spend a weekend in her home. She developed a bond with Dunia through our calls—Dunia trusted her enough to open up, and I knew that the true meaning of Dunia's words were coming through to me from Nazek's translations.

Once Nazek began translating for us, my relationship with Dunia began to deepen. Through Nazek's beautiful, soothing voice, I truly felt I was speaking directly to Dunia for the first time.

It was also Nazek who suggested an alternative to our unreliable phone connections. "Why don't we try Viber?" she said.

"What's that?" I asked.

Nazek explained that Viber is a group texting app she used to communicate with her family overseas. It uses data or Wi-Fi instead of a cellular connection. And as long as we were connecting to another Viber user, the calls were free. The best part was that it allowed not only written text messages and photos but also thirty-second recorded audio or video messages. So, I could see Dunia's face and hear her voice talking or singing, which was so important to me.

We were able to set up a three-way Viber conversation with Nazek, so that Dunia could write messages or post recordings in Arabic, and Nazek would write or record translations for me. It allowed us to have regular calls or video calls, too, but we still faced the difficulty of spotty connections and time differences.

To make it happen, we had to get Dunia an iPad—something with a bigger screen that was easier to use than a phone. I sent money to Mo and asked him to buy the iPad, facilitate getting it to Dunia, and make sure it had an Arabic keyboard and the right charging cords.

From the time of that first message I received from Dunia, her world opened up to me, and her stories came to life.

CHAPTER 26

DUNIA: WHAT IS THIS LIFE?

What happened on that day is a thing that never will be removed or erased. Never, ever, ever. How can I forget the most painful moment in the whole world? How can I forget when I close my eyes and I see my son in my head? When I came to say goodbye to him, and I tried to sniff him or to hug him, I can smell only the burn of his body. And when I smelled the burn of his body, all the milk in my breasts came out.

It was on November 29, 2003. They were going to a doctor, but at the same time they wanted to go shopping. Yousif asked his dad for a bike. The agreement was, they would finish the doctor appointment and then finish their shopping, and then they would go and buy a bike for Yousif. Everything else I have tried to forget from that day on. But these days will be never forgotten. They are engraved in my heart, and in my soul, and in all my body. I will never forget these days.

When I held their hands, my boy and my girl, the blood started dripping, and I started wiping my body with their blood from my head to toe. I couldn't hold them because it was all blood and burns. I started screaming—screaming with all my voice. Maybe he will return to me. My boy Yousif will hear my voice and return to me. Maybe God will hear my loudest voice and He will have mercy on me and return my boy to me.

But He didn't hear me.

I loved my boy, and he left me, and all the sorrow and sadness eats me from inside. Two lovely young children playing together, sleeping together, dreaming together, they do everything together. They walk together, they do everything together. And then all of a sudden, death separates them from being together.

What is this life? What is this world?

I cried for the soul of my son for days and weeks. I went to his grave and cried on his grave. I lit candles because he is scared of darkness. I never returned home; I stayed at his grave for days and nights. I never left him. I left my daughter and I stayed with Yousif. Because he is scared of the dark, and I cannot leave him in the dark.

All of a sudden I said, "Oh, my God, I have a daughter!" And my daughter, she cannot see me like that. She's also sick, and she's also burned! Just as Yousif left me, I am leaving my daughter, so she will leave me also. No, I have to return to my daughter and take care of her.

That was the worst day of my life when I left Yousif, but I must go back home to take care of Teeba. I have to say goodbye to Yousif and go back to Teeba.

I started worrying about my daughter, about my daughter dying. The doctors were telling me, "She's not going to survive." Then, the hectic days and the worst days of my life started. Hospitals, doctors without ending. Our lives got harder and harder—as if it wasn't hard enough. And I say, "What kind of life am I living?" It makes me feel that I'm done; I'm done with this life. I cannot take it anymore, and the time is not worth it. But I need to fight for the sake of my daughter.

I try sometimes not to remember these days, but then I remember. I can never stop remembering. Every single word aches my heart. Every single word, the scar is open.

My daughter Teeba would look at me and say, "Why are you sad? Why are you crying all the time? Why is the pillow wet, Mommy?" In Iraq we would sleep on the roof when it is hot, and Teeba would try to count the stars. She starts giggling and laughing, a very innocent baby, and she turns to me and sees me crying. She tries to wipe my tears, and says, "Are you not happy with me because I don't know how to count? Please teach me how to count the stars. I don't want you to be upset with me because I don't know how to count the stars."

Then I started, for the sake of Teeba, to draw the smile on my face. I wanted her to come back to me and not to be scared of me. But my heart is still bleeding for Yousif. I started running with her, eating with her, playing with her, and little by little she started coming back to me again. I started smelling her again and hugging her again.

I lose a son, and then I leave my daughter when she is five years old. I had to. I didn't have any other choice, and I know it is best for her. When the time came for Teeba to leave, she was crying a lot. She was holding my hand and crying to her dad, saying, "I don't want to leave my mom. I don't want to go." Furat had to pull her out of my lap. She even caught Fatima's hand. "I don't want to leave Mom. I don't want to leave Fatima. I want to stay home. Don't take me away from here."

I still remember the look in her eyes—the sight of the door before it was closed. She's the little girl I had to let go.

At that time, I hated myself. I felt broken. I felt useless. I hated my life. I was even asking God, "Why? Why me? Why is all of this happening to me? What am I supposed to do? What can I do?" People think I don't have a heart. No, I have a heart, I have really a big heart, but a heart that absorbed all the sadness, a heart that can store all this for the sake of my daughter.

Teeba, honey, I wish I could have prevented you from getting in the accident. I wish I could take you and put you back in my belly where nothing can happen to you. It's not something I control. It's destiny. It's meant to happen. And this is life, it's a lot of hard, hard things that you have to deal with. We have to deal with it and we have to learn from it and move on. Don't ever think I would not have prevented the pain if I could. I would prevent it with all my heart, with all my life.

I don't know how long I'm going to live and if I'm ever going to see you again. This is why I'm writing, just in case I never see you. If I die, you get to know the stories of your life firsthand. From me.

I never loved anyone like Teeba. It's true I do have girls and a boy, and I love them. But not like Teeba. She is the one who is far away from me; she's the one I cannot smell; she's the one I cannot hug. I wish and dream that one day I can put her back on my lap. I can hug her again, and I can put her on my chest to sleep like when she was a baby.

I don't know if this day will ever come.

Teeba, if I'm shopping, I feel sad because I want to buy you clothes the same way I used to. When I bathe Fatima and Maryam, I hold my tears because I remember bathing you. I don't want the girls to see me crying. I always imagine you in my hands when I comb their hair and dry them out after their baths. You always wanted to do a different hairstyle every day. When it's Eid, which is our holiday, the first gift I prepare is Teeba's gift, even though she's not here. Teeba is with us all the time even though she's not with us.

When I used to wash your clothes, you'd come and play with me in the soap foam. It's like a movie in my head. Every time I do something, I remember exactly how we used to play together. Every day this movie is repeated in my head over and over. When I miss you, I go to your clothing from when you were little and try to smell it. That makes me feel good.

I still see you as the baby who left me. I can't see you as a grown-up. I see you like the flower before it's blossomed, the jasmine flower. I see you like the colorful baby bird, flying from one tree to the other. I see you like a butterfly flying from one tree to the other.

I miss you as much as the dry land misses the water. I miss you as much as the big sky in America pours rain on you. I can't even describe to you how much I love you. It's beyond any words that can be said.

Yesterday I hoped that the phone call that we had together wouldn't end. I was so happy to see you. I know you didn't talk a lot, Teeba, but I didn't care about you talking. I just wanted to keep looking at you. You are so, so, so beautiful. I was really happy to see your eyes.

I noticed a very shy look in your eyes. It's a sparkle in your eyes. I love that. I really do.

You know the night before when I went to bed? I took the iPad with me. I was hugging the iPad when I'm sleeping because I was imagining you. I was imagining the iPad was you, and I'm sleeping and hugging you with me. I wish that night doesn't end because I was so happy, so excited to see you. When I saw you, I felt like I don't need to do anything.

I know you can't feel the same way, but I'm dreaming about the day and the time that I can see you. I don't know if I'll ever be able to see you, but you're always in my heart. You're always in my thinking. I think about you all the time.

Teeba, we sent gifts to you. I hope you like them. I bought you earrings, and I want you to wear them all the time so you can remember me each time they touch your beautiful cheeks. I have a small box where I saved everything you had before you left, and I always go to the box and I remember you as I kiss them.

I feel a little guilty that I'm not with you through everything you're going through. I will send you a Koran and I want you to put it under your pillow when you sleep. As I write this, my tears cannot stop coming out. I can't wait for the day when I'll surround you with my arms and my warm chest. I've been counting the hours to see you and kiss you and sleep next to you and sing for you.

I hope you're not going to forget your mom.

One day when Teeba was little I went with Furat to Baghdad to see a doctor. On our way, we went to visit a holy shrine. That day it was raining hard. I always used to wear an abaya, and I used to keep Teeba underneath my abaya to cover her from the rain. When we got inside the shrine, Teeba wanted to get down. She got down on the floor under my abaya, and in a little while I could feel that Teeba wasn't there. I was so scared. We were looking all over. We couldn't find her. We were afraid we had lost Teeba.

Finally, we found her with a Lebanese lady who came with the American soldiers. She was standing next to the place where they sell abayas, and Teeba was trying to buy one because she wanted to cover my head.

This is Teeba. Even when she was little, she's so considerate. She wanted to cover my head and protect me from the rain. The Lebanese lady who came with the American soldiers already bought her the abaya, and we got her back. Always when I see the American soldiers, I feel safe and comfortable. They always have helped me and Teeba.

One night, when we were sleeping on the roof, Teeba asked, "Can I fly to the moon?" She always thought that I have a magic wand, so I say, "Yes, close your eyes and I will take you up to the moon, and we will fly together using my magic wand."

One day when her dad came back home, she was telling him I had a magic wand and every day we fly to the moon. Furat had a big laugh.

"Really? Your mom has a magic wand? Can you guys take me with you? I want to go with you to the moon." Teeba looked at him and said, "No, we can't take you to the moon. It's only for princesses."

Teeba, do you remember that? Do you still love the moon? Do you remember when we were up on the roof and I held you until you fell asleep, and we'd pretend that we both went to the moon? I wish I had a magic wand where I can just wiggle it and be by you and hug you and take you to my chest.

When we had a nice day, I would tell her, "You are my moon." If she was sad, I would tell her, "You are the wounded moon today." When she was happy, I would tell her, "You're the loving moon today." And when her eye sparkled, I would tell her, "You're the glowing moon today."

The moon is so far away and I cannot reach it, and so is Teeba now.

All of these stories I'm telling you, most of it Furat doesn't know. I hate telling him things that will make him upset or have extra burdens on him on top of his work and everything else. My life has so many bad stories, and the one bright thing in my life is Furat. I love him dearly.

When Furat comes home from the army, I clean the house like it's a holiday cleaning. I cook the best food for him that he enjoys. When he comes home, I feel like a newlywed. I forget the whole world. All the sorrow, all the bad things. And this is why most of these stories, Furat doesn't know about. Furat promised me he will never let me cry when we got married. My life is full of sorrow and I cry a lot, but if he sees me crying, he's heartbroken.

When Furat is not with me, I feel broken. I feel lost. I always thought I'm strong and tall, like a big, tall palm tree. But in reality this tall palm tree is hollow inside and cannot stand any wind and cannot stand tall. I don't feel strong. I feel this type of life turned my bones into dust. I'm so fragile, so broken apart. So this is why I hide it from him. I don't want him to feel that I am hurting.

When Furat comes home, I have so much joy and happiness, I can't even explain it. He is my first and last love. I love the earth he walks on. I don't want anyone to even hurt him with a word. It's unexplainable. He's always good to me and takes care of me. He is my angel.

CHAPTER 27

TEEBA: A SECOND CHANCE

As I got older, I began to feel God nudging me to give my biological family another chance. Maybe they deserved more than empty conversation on the phone. Maybe they want more than my emotional distance. Maybe today will be the last day either of my parents takes a breath.

I knew it was time to open up to my family, but little did I know they would open up to me, too, and make me fall in love with each of them. The more I spoke with my mom Dunia, the more it felt like nothing had really changed. As soon as I started to speak to my mom again, the news channel was no longer background noise while I did my homework; it became the quickest way to make sure my family was safe. Racist slurs became more and more difficult to rub off, because it was one thing to attack me for my beliefs and background, but it was an entirely different game when someone attacked my family. And mostly, prayer became a way for me to thank God for all I had rather than ask for all I wanted.

My mom Dunia speaks in a soft voice that could calm even the nerves of someone on death row. It's a tone that feels comforting. I could always understand when she was complimenting me, or when she was talking about my siblings, and I was able to understand when she's talking about her health, mainly because she'll use words like *inshallah* ("God willing") or *alḥamdulillāh* ("all praise is due to God alone") or *subhaṅu wa'tala Allah* ("the most glorified Allah").

I was pretty young when I got my green card, but I understood it would be a way for me to stay in America. As long as I could still call the woman who gave birth to me "mom," I had no real concerns. The entire process, however, was not one I could truly be grateful for as a child. Even now, it's hard to understand just how great of a blessing it is and what an honor it is to be part of this country.

I have always been very proud of my background, even if people make me think I shouldn't be. My country, my families, and my culture mean everything to me. I thought, however, if I live on the other side of the world, and my lifestyle is completely changed, what proof do I even have that I started out where I did? Almost every aspect of my life had been changed and flipped upside down. I hoped none of my family back home would resent me, that my mom and dad over there would still proudly call me their daughter, and that I'd still be recognized for who I began as and flourished into, not just the person I am right now.

As I've said before, my heart and mind have always been conflicted between speaking my mind and just saying what everyone wants to hear. But it's become more and more evident to me that if I have a real contribution to make, it's only right that I share it. I've learned that an opinion is better said starting with "I" rather than "you." I've learned that there is nothing more blissful than listening more than you talk.

With these little philosophies I live by, I realized that as long as I keep the mindset I have, and put God and family above all worldly goods, goals, and ambitions, no legal transaction can tear any aspect of my life apart. It's my responsibility to keep it together, and no force on earth can divide this world greater than a loss of faith. Like I always say, if God didn't want to see me right here, He would have stopped me a long time ago.

When I heard my mom Dunia's stories through Viber, I started to feel more and more that I wanted to see her again. But when I thought about that meeting, I suddenly began to worry about how my mom would react to my new lifestyle. How would she react if she noticed I occasionally miss one or two of the daily prayers? How would she react to me not wearing a hijab?

But the biggest thing that bothered me was that I was scared my mom wouldn't think I was beautiful. I didn't want her to think all these surgeries were a waste of time. I wanted to show my mom she made the right decision, through my "new" skin and my renewed attitude toward my circumstances.

The reason this mattered to me so much was because my mom Dunia knew that, in the beginning, I was angry at what happened to me. I knew she remembered me crying to her about my frail hair constantly falling out and my scabbed head continually bleeding. But ever since I was three or four years old, I realized the more I treated my circumstances like they were the end of the world, the more she fell apart as well.

With the death of my brother, the constant agony I felt at the slightest touch of my skin, and the pain of being rejected by other children, I found it difficult to stop myself from crying whenever I saw my reflection. But even then, I saw that my mom needed to know I was content with the situation in order to create a sense of closure between herself and the accident that took her son away from her and my childhood away from me. So I would wipe my tears away, then wipe hers away.

I wanted my mom to see me and to know that I don't have to convince her anymore that I feel beautiful. I just wanted her to see it. I wanted her to look at me and know that she made the right decision letting me go to America and allowing me to take on this new life.

CHAPTER 28

THE JOURNEY HOME

In March 2016, we got devastating news from Iraq. Tearfully, Dunia told Nazek that she'd visited her doctor complaining of vision problems. After running tests the doctors suspected there might be a tumor growing behind her eye. They were recommending surgery, but there was a real possibility that she would lose her eyesight if the surgery went wrong.

Dunia had seen several doctors, but she always received conflicting information and varying diagnoses. She'd been delaying having the surgery, hoping she would have the chance to lay eyes on Teeba one more time.

This news struck me right in the gut. Over the nine years Teeba had been in the United States, we'd continued to struggle with how and when we could reunite Teeba with her family in a way that wouldn't risk her safety, her immigration status, or her medical treatments. But now I knew what had to happen. We simply could not take the risk that Dunia might lose her vision without seeing the beautiful young woman Teeba had grown up to be.

Tim and I were distressed thinking that Dunia's last vision of Teeba would be of a scarred and scared little five-year-old child crying in fear about leaving her home and family. Our intermittent Viber or FaceTime calls were no longer enough. There was a sense of urgency—Dunia had to see her daughter *now*.

One of our worries had already been alleviated—now that Teeba was a legal permanent resident, we could travel outside the United States without fear that she might not be able to get back in. But the continued violence in Iraq made a trip there out of the question for us, and Dunia was still insisting that I never let Teeba return for her own safety.

Unfortunately, getting Dunia to the United States for a visit would have been next to impossible. The process of applying for a visa to enter the United States is slow and expensive, and her chances of obtaining approval were slim. Demonstrating intent to return to your home country is a critical part of the visa approval process, and Dunia's circumstances—having a daughter in the United States from whom she'd been separated for nine years—would have raised suspicion with USCIS that she might overstay her visa. It would have raised even more red flags if she applied to bring along her other children.

So we couldn't go to them, and they couldn't come to us. How on earth could we make this reunion happen?

It was Nazek who suggested we return to the idea we'd briefly considered in 2008. "What if you met them in Jordan?" she said. "It would be easier for Dunia to reach Jordan, and it would be safer for you there." Nazek even offered to meet us there and help with translation. Just as important, Steve Sosebee and Mo Khudairi both had offices in Jordan's capital, Amman, and they agreed that Jordan would be a much safer option than going to Iraq.

That settled it.

Tim and I started our initial research and planning, but we kept it a secret. We didn't tell Teeba about her mother's vision problems, and we wanted to wait as long as possible to tell her about the trip. We didn't want to get her hopes up only to have the plans fall apart, like they had back in 2008.

I remember asking Tim what he thought about the idea of going to the Middle East, and especially the cost of bringing in her mother and three siblings. "Honey, if we can make this happen, we have to," he said. "It always works out somehow. God has always provided the way."

What I didn't know at the time was that Teeba had begun privately to feel a strong desire to see her family again. There were so many years we had to force her to get on the phone with her parents. It was a fight to get her to say something, even if it was in English, or at least sing—anything that would allow Dunia to hear her voice.

But at around twelve years old, Teeba began to feel a renewed connection to her Iraqi family, especially as she listened to Dunia talk about life in Iraq in her own voice through Viber.

One of the turning points came in 2014, when Dunia became pregnant with twins. Teeba was twelve, and old enough to pay attention to and understand her mother's stories. While she was pregnant, Dunia learned that one of her cousins had been killed by a suicide bomber while coming out of a mosque, and she said the stress of that news caused her to lose one of the twins, a girl. Dunia went to the doctor, who said the second child was a boy and appeared to be healthy. But then Dunia began to bleed, and felt in her gut that something was wrong with the baby. She asked the doctor to do her C-section early, but he insisted on more money before he would do the surgery. So she found a second doctor who agreed to deliver the baby.

Just as Dunia had feared, the baby was born with severe lung problems and was immediately whisked away to be put on a respirator. The hospital forced Dunia to go home because of security concerns, but the baby stayed in intensive care. Shortly thereafter, he died.

Amal was the one who retrieved the baby from the hospital and prepared him for burial. Dunia never got to see her baby—only a picture many months later that Amal had taken at the hospital.

Stories like these touched our hearts so deeply. Teeba began to see the life she was missing. I've learned since that it's common for kids separated from their parents to reach a turning point around that age, but Teeba kept all of those feelings to herself.

One night in April, while we were in the midst of secret planning for our trip to Jordan, Teeba and I had an argument. I don't remember what it was about—probably one of those typical fights that teenage girls have with their moms. She ran up to her room crying, and I followed her. I could sense she was holding something back from me. Finally, in a burst of emotion, she said the words she'd been holding inside for so long.

"I want to see my mom," Teeba cried out. "I want to see my family. I would do whatever it takes to get one more hug from my mom. But I didn't want to say it because I didn't want to upset you."

"Oh, honey, I'm not upset," I said. I sat next to her on the bed as my own tears began to flow freely. "I wouldn't have been upset by that. I think it's wonderful that you want to see her. I want to see her too."

"I know you're afraid that I'll want to go back," Teeba said. "I miss my mom, and I would go back to Iraq to see her if I had to. But I don't want to stay."

I couldn't keep our secret any longer. "We're going to see your mom and siblings in Jordan," I stated calmly. Then I waited, holding my breath.

Teeba went silent and looked up at me. "Are you serious?"

"Yes. We've been working for a while to arrange this trip, but we didn't want to get your hopes up until we knew it would happen."

Teeba jumped to her feet and shrieked in excitement. Her tears vanished and she bounded over to hug me tight.

"I love you, honey," I said as I held her. "We're going to make this happen for you."

Teeba and I headed downstairs and opened up my laptop. She immediately began searching for information on Jordan, pulling up striking images of Jordan's most famous landmarks like the Petra World Heritage Site, where the ruins of an ancient city are carved into the rose-red rock, plus Amman's Roman amphitheater and the Dead Sea.

Teeba scanned and clicked, reading off various facts about Jordan with a broad smile on her face. We'd spent nearly nine years talking about making this reunion happen someday, but now someday was finally going to become a reality.

It had to.

Sitting in my dining room one evening, Nazek and I called Dunia. I could barely contain myself as we went through our usual greetings.

"Dunia, we're coming to see you," I said, choking back tears. "You're finally going to get to see Teeba!"

I waited a moment while Nazek translated, then I heard Dunia shout in joy and immediately burst into tears. Nazek tried to keep up while the two of us—each in our own languages—sobbed and shared our feelings of love and excitement. We couldn't help but allow our fears to sneak into our conversation. Dunia immediately worried that her mother-in-law would try to stop her from making the trip, or that a complication would arise on our end, or that she wouldn't be able to get out of the country, even though Amman was within driving distance of the village.

Still, her message to us was clear: she would let nothing stand in the way of seeing Teeba again.

As we continued to plan and prepare, however, one of Mo's colleagues gave us bad news—the Jordanian government was no longer allowing Iraqis to drive across the border due to the risk of car and suicide bombings.

I called Mo, devastated.

"I promised Teeba and Dunia I would make this happen," I told him. "What am I going to do?"

He suggested a Plan B—meeting Dunia and the kids in Dubai. Part of the United Arab Emirates, Dubai is located on the Persian Gulf and is one of the top five travel destinations in the world. Almost fifteen million people visit the country every year. Mo was living in Dubai at the time and said he could be there to help us and translate during our trip. Nazek agreed that Dubai would be a perfect location, plus she offered to also meet us there and connected us with her cousin in Baghdad who was a travel agent and could help with the logistics. That option also made getting Dunia and her kids there easier—if we purchased tickets through Emirates Air, the company would facilitate getting the necessary visas. Tim agreed that we should do whatever it took to get them there easily and safely.

I called Dunia and told her about the change of plans, and the vice grip I felt in my chest released. I had no idea how much fear and anxiety I'd been feeling traveling to Jordan, so close to the most violent parts of the Middle East, until I finally exhaled. The prospect of traveling to the Middle East still terrified me, but I began to let some of that fear dissolve into excitement. Teeba was elated, and she stepped into the mother role, trying to reassure me and ease my fears.

The months of preparation before our trip to Dubai were emotionally overwhelming. Just as I had back when I was trying to bring Teeba to America, I flung myself into research, posting requests for information online, making phone calls to connect with anyone who had traveled to Dubai, and then drilling them unmercifully with questions. We heard glowing reports about the welcoming people, the beautiful scenery, and the amazing sightseeing.

Our commitment to seeing Dunia started to feel real once I started verbalizing it to other people. Thinking about it and talking about it at home was one thing, but telling others gave it substance and life. One of the first people I called was my close friend and senior partner at the law firm I work for, Pat Perotti.

"Hi, Pat, I just wanted to let you know that I'm going to be taking a week of vacation time in July," I said.

"What? Where are you going?" Pat seemed surprised. We'd worked together for eight years by that time, and our families had bonded instantly. Pat, his wife, Sharon, and daughter, Mary, are the kind of people who, once you become a friend, make you instantly part of their family.

We'd taken many of our family vacations with them over the years, so I'm sure the idea of us traveling without him made him more than a little curious.

"We're finally going to meet Teeba's mom and sisters and brother!" I said excitedly. I'd previously mentioned that we were working to try to reunite them, but this was the first time he was hearing the trip was finally going to happen.

"What!" he yelled into the phone. "You're going to Dubai? You settled on Dubai? You're going to see Teeba's family? We're in. We're going with you. And we aren't going for one week, we're going for two. You can't go that far just for one week."

At first I was resistant. I worried that having so many people there might be too overwhelming for Dunia. But I knew that having the Perottis there would help give us some support and levity during what would be an emotional week. Teeba calls them Uncle Pat and Aunt Sharon, and considers Mary—five years older than her—like a big sister. Pat is like a big kid, and he's always up to go anywhere and do anything. He's Teeba's go-to person for intellectual banter, and they're constantly quizzing each other about random things like the elements of the periodic table or the books of the Bible. Sharon has a deep faith and has always provided a steady, stable force in Teeba's life. She struggles with a vision impairment, and Teeba is always right there to lend a hand.

So Pat became my planning partner for the trip, and we went on a mission to create a jam-packed itinerary of activities. Teeba and I shopped for presents to take to Dunia and the kids, and I got emotional with each gift I picked out. Just like the teddy bear I bought for Teeba when she first arrived in the United States, I wanted every gift to be perfect—things that they could take back home to their village to remember our time together.

In the months preceding our trip to the Middle East, I obsessed about nightmarish stories I heard about the rules and regulations in place concerning the behavior and appearance of tourists in Dubai. I tried to go shopping for conservative clothing, but I agonized over every detail of my packing list. Financially, the trip was well beyond our means since we were paying all of the travel expenses for Teeba's family too. The process of getting visas for Dunia and the kids went smoothly, but Furat was denied. That's not uncommon since he served in the Iraqi military, but we worried that he might not allow his wife and children to make the trip alone.

Then, just a few weeks before the trip, Nazek called.

"Barbara, I have some bad news," she said. "I can't come with you to Dubai."

"What? Please, don't tell me that, Nazek," I said. "I can't do this without you."

Over the years that she had been translating in my conversations with Dunia on Viber, the three of us had become very close, sharing our secrets and giggling like teenage girls. I had envisioned us staying up late into the night in Dubai, talking and bonding despite the language barrier. Nazek was my lifeline to Dunia.

The problem was that she'd recently moved to Kuwait to care for her ailing father and was searching for a new job there.

"I was looking forward to the three of us finally being together too," she said. "But I would be in violation of my resident visa if I left Kuwait, and I can't take the risk of not being able to get back into the country. I'll still be in the same time zone, so we can call and FaceTime."

Nazek's suggestion of using Viber, and her translations over those years, were the biggest reasons that I'd been able to finally build a relationship with Dunia. It's what propelled us from dreaming about someday reuniting her with Teeba to becoming motivated to figure out how to make it happen now. Nazek was the one who gave me the courage to make this trip happen, despite all of my worries and fears. I was disappointed that she couldn't be there, but I was also worried about how this would impact our communication with Dunia while we were there. Dunia trusted Nazek. She might not open up with another translator, especially if it was a man.

More personal fears swirled in my head too: Would Dunia like us? What would the kids be like? How would Teeba feel being with two mothers? Would there be a feeling of competition between us? What if Dunia insisted on taking Teeba home with her? That fear was mixed with shame—here I was, worried that Teeba's own mother might want to take her away from me.

Despite Teeba's reassurance, my biggest unspoken fear still was: *Would Teeba want to go back to Iraq?*

Somehow, some way, God cleared our path, as He always does. Being the kind and loving man that he is, Furat encouraged his family to make the trip. Mo stepped up to offer help with translation and logistics in Nazek's absence. Always my voice of reason, Tim had a great attitude and put his personal fears and anxieties to rest for the moment. Teeba was excited, and the Perottis were standing by to provide not only the emotional support we needed, but also the spiritual support and strength we would desperately require.

Just a few days before we left, I received a bouquet of flowers from my friend Audry. The card read: "Those chills and butterflies you are feeling aren't nerves. They're the tickle of the feathers of angels as they ready their wings to wrap you in protection for your travels. Agape, Audry."

Her message brought calm to my soul. *Agape* is love and faith, commitment and willfulness. It's the type of love that is so beautifully described in 1 Corinthians 13:

> Love is patient, love is kind. It does not envy, it does not boast, it is not proud. It does not dishonor others, it is not self-seeking, it is not easily angered, it keeps no record of wrongs. Love does not delight in evil but rejoices with the truth. It always protects, always trusts, always hopes, always perseveres. (vv. 4–7)

I tucked that card into my suitcase to bring with me to Dubai.

As she often does, Teeba also provided me with comfort I needed as I spent that final night packing and fretting. "Mom, don't worry. Nothing is going to happen. God wouldn't have brought me all this way to have something bad happen to us now. Everything always turns out okay."

She was right. Her words helped me turn a corner away from my worries and toward hope. I captured that moment in my heart. As we left the house for the airport on the morning of July 6, 2016, I thought back to the day we drove to the same airport to meet Teeba for the first time, almost exactly nine years before. I knew that the moment we got on that plane, I would once again be forever changed.

CHAPTER 29

DUNIA: I TRY MY BEST

ife is full of terror. Without this terror, you wouldn't feel happiness. This is how life gets balanced. You have to have happy times and sad times. It's unfortunate that I had so much sad time, but I still love my life. I never told anyone my stories or my sadness.

Barbara, you and Nazek are the only two I can open up to. When I feel the need to talk to someone, I look at the stars and talk to the stars as if they are listening. When a star moves or goes away or sparkles, it feels like the star heard me—that makes me feel good.

The children have a lot of things they would like to do and enjoy. Rides, outings, things I cannot give them given the security issues and the country being in constant war. The kids were very happy to see the pictures of Teeba at the zoo with the animals, so they say, "Mom, why can't we go and play like Teeba?" It's not easy to explain to them the circumstances in our country.

I try my best.

This year, three days before Eid, I went to buy groceries and chicken for the holiday. I took Aboody with me in the store, but Aboody saw the bicycle shop next door. Aboody loves bicycles, so he asks me if he can go and see the bikes. He was upset because I promised to buy him a bike two years ago, and it never happened. I felt bad that he's been looking at these bikes and I still cannot afford buying him the bike. I said to myself, "At least let him enjoy looking at the bicycles."

I was trying to pay at the grocery store when I noticed that I can't see him anymore. At that moment, a bomb went off. Everybody was running all over the place, and ambulances came, and I couldn't see anything. I was shouting from the top of my lungs for Aboody, but I can't see him. Luckily I heard his voice calling, "Mom, mom, I'm here," so I ran toward the sound.

The bomb threw him away from where I was looking for him. I was so glad to find him, but he couldn't open his eyes, and he didn't want to even speak to me. I picked him up and ran with him to the hospital. Once the doctors stitched his head and his hands, I took him back home.

When Furat called home to check on me and the girls, he asked about Aboody. I told him he's playing outside in the street with the kids. The first couple days, Aboody wasn't able to talk even, so once he was able to talk again, I got Aboody to tell his dad he was playing in the street—this is why he didn't talk to him. When Furat heard Aboody's voice, he was comfortable that everything is okay.

Thank you for the [elementary school] graduation pictures. The night before, I was dreaming that you were angry and mad because I wanted you to give me all the certificates for Teeba's school so I could frame them and hang them. In the dream, you said, "How dare you ask such a thing?" You said Teeba is your daughter and you should keep all her certificates!

Then I woke up and here I see all of the pictures and certificates from Teeba's graduation. I was laughing so hard at myself. I am so thankful to you. It's as if you're really living inside me!

The thing that is even more beautiful than the pictures is the relationship between you and Teeba. I can tell from these pictures you have a special bond with Teeba, and this is really a good thing for me.

Barbara, I'm confident you will raise and care for Teeba better than anyone on this world. You've seen so much in your life, you know how hard life can be. If anything happens to me, I'm going to be comfortable because you love my daughter and I know Teeba is with you. You will take good care of her. You will always remind her of me. You will always tell her not to forget me. And you will tell her all the stories about me.

You will tell Teeba that I never betrayed her—never left her. I encouraged Furat to get her out of the country because I want her to have a better life than mine.

There are not enough words to say thank you. Thank you is a drop in an ocean, and you, Barbara, are the ocean. Your love, your caring for me and my daughter, is beyond any words of thanks.

Teeba, honey, I'm your mom. I understand what you want even if I don't talk to you. It's true that I'm away from you and I haven't seen you for a while, but you're still my daughter. I still understand you without saying a word.

Please listen to your mom Barbara. She loves you. She cares for you. She's the one who feels your pain. All your memories with me, Teeba, were a lot of problems. But your memories with Mama Barbara are full of fun and good things that you can remember.

CHAPTER 30

REUNION

Stepping off the plane into the Dubai airport was like entering a palace. The terminal looked more like a lavish Las Vegas resort than an airport, with towering white columns, lush indoor palm trees, massive water features, mirrored walls and ceilings, and pristine marble floors. Everything was immaculately clean, and everyone was crisply dressed.

The thirteen-hour flight had been a blur. We were packed into a two-story Emirates plane that held more than six hundred people. It was quieter in the back of the plane where Tim, Teeba, and Mary were sitting, but Pat, Sharon, and I were stuck in the midsection amidst chaos—people chattering in a multitude of languages, babies crying, and cramped space. I was so tired from all the preparations, but it was hard for me to breathe, much less sleep or even read.

Plus, endless thoughts and expectations kept rattling around in my brain in anticipation of meeting Dunia. I tried to imagine how she was feeling at that moment. Was she having many of the same fears and excitements as I was? She'd never been on a plane and she'd never left Iraq, let alone traveled with three children and without her husband.

In my head I kept trying to plan out how this moment of reunion would happen. But I had to remind myself—as I often do—that we plan and God laughs!

The six of us couldn't wait to disembark as soon as the wheels hit the ground. As tired as we were, the opulence of the airport had our bleary eyes wide and our mouths agape. The Emirati women at the customs entry were stunning, like they'd just stepped out of a magazine. Their faces were works of art. The woman who reviewed our passports was about five feet, six inches, slim, and dressed in a black hijab framing her face; the black abaya she wore was made of a stunning fabric that flowed around her body. Her fingernails were perfectly manicured and painted, and her impeccable makeup had me transfixed.

"Excuse me, but you are really beautiful," said Tim to the gorgeous customs agent. This was typical Tim—he has always been flirtatious but never in a way that's disrespectful to me. Tim is gregarious and warm, and he never hesitates to compliment the people around him. Even if he is in a foreign country with very different views about treatment of women.

She thanked him and smiled politely, but I was mortified. We were barely off the plane twenty minutes and I was already visualizing us—or at least Tim—getting arrested for sexually harassing an Emirati woman. Once we were out of earshot of the customs agent, I threatened him with his life if he ever did that again. I reminded him that we were not on American soil any longer, and we had to watch our boundaries.

After retrieving our six huge pieces of luggage, we headed for the door. Stepping into the 115-degree Dubai heat in July was like entering a blast furnace. It isn't dry heat, either—the humidity that day got up to 75 percent. You could see the heat rising from the sidewalks and floating away through the air. We waited for a vehicle that could accommodate our crowd and our massive heap of baggage, then piled in and headed off to the apartment I'd reserved for two weeks. As we drove, we craned our necks to take in our first glimpses of the city.

Without a doubt, Dubai is the cleanest city I have ever seen—almost as if there are invisible cleaning people everywhere. The roads were perfectly clean and smooth, and we learned that residents can be fined for having a dirty car. All the signs were in English as well as Arabic, which was a relief for me. As we passed downtown Dubai, we saw towering buildings that gleamed in the sunlight unlike anything any of us had ever seen before. Cranes stretched toward the sky where new skyscrapers would soon join them.

We arrived at the hotel exhausted and staggered out of the van. We'd rented an apartment attached to the Adagio Premium Dubai Al Barsha hotel. It was forty-one floors, and every apartment was shaped like the bow of a boat, jutting out of the building's facade, allowing us a nearly 180-degree view. We dragged ourselves into the elevator and up to the twenty-seventh floor, desperate for a place to crash. But our exhaustion didn't keep us from being wowed by the view from the floor-to-ceiling windows looking out over the outskirts of Dubai. It was strange to see so much sand and concrete, with little foliage. In the distance, we could see the Burj Al Arab, known as one of the most luxurious hotels in the world and one of the most iconic features of the Dubai skyline—a towering hotel built to resemble a sail on a mast sitting on its own man-made island in the Persian Gulf.

Our view of everything was hazy. It was like looking through dirty eyeglasses, and we instinctively squinted, trying to see better. Pat pulled out his phone to check the weather app, hoping that the haze might clear in the coming days so we could get a better view of the Burj Al Arab. As he scrolled through the week's forecast, Pat burst out laughing.

"What? What does it say?" I headed to look over Pat's shoulder.

Instead of seeing "sunny" or "rainy" like we would back home, the forecast just said "DUST." And there would be no letting up, either—it would be 119 degrees and DUST the entire week.

The apartment was perfect for our reunion with Dunia and the kids. It had four bedrooms with four full and two half bathrooms, a large kitchen, a laundry room, and wide-open living spaces. One bedroom and bathroom were separated from the others down a hall, allowing Dunia extra privacy, which was especially important for a Muslim woman traveling without her husband.

We had a few hours to kill before Dunia and the kids arrived, and everyone wanted to get some sleep and get cleaned up. Pat and Sharon headed off to their room, and Teeba and Mary off to theirs. I showered and tried to make myself presentable, as exhausted and weepy as I was, then joined Tim walking across the street to a small grocery to pick up drinks, bread, water, fruits, and other snacks.

When we got back to the apartment, I tried to rest, but I knew there was no way I'd fall asleep. I lay there on the bed, restless and stewing in thoughts of this reunion, my adrenaline and my heart racing. Teeba seemed cool and calm, but I knew in her heart she was feeling anxiety, excitement, and most of all love, thinking about seeing her mother for the first time in nine years—thinking about what it would mean to have two moms together in one place. She's not often open with her emotions, but I knew she'd been worried. She wanted her mother to think she was pretty.

Soon I gave up on trying to sleep, wandered out alone into the living room, and sat down on the enormous couch, upholstered in soft tan fabric and piled high with pillows. The whole apartment was quiet, and I squeezed one of those pillows to my chest, gazing out the window over the dusty Dubai landscape. But I couldn't stay seated—I'd jump up within moments and wander to another part of the apartment. I unpacked the gifts we'd brought for Dunia, the kids, and Mo, then arranged and rearranged them on decorative shelves in the dining room. I poured candy and bubble gum into bowls. Then rearranged the gifts again.

My heart felt full to bursting. This was the moment I'd dreamed of for years—all those times I walked the halls of the hospital at 3:00 a.m., pushing Teeba in her wheelchair past the windows of the skywalk, telling her that her mother was looking up at the same stars. All the years of struggling to communicate with Dunia through spotty phone connections and language barriers, never knowing if my love for her and my gratitude for her sacrifice were getting through. All the stories of her life that had finally burst into technicolor thanks to Nazek and Viber.

Yes, Teeba was being reunited with her mother, but I felt like I was being reunited with someone I'd never met yet loved like a daughter. Like a sister.

The apartment gradually began to stir—it was nearly time, and everyone was pulling themselves out of the haze of their naps. We were waiting for a text from Mo, who was picking up Dunia, Fatima, Maryam, and Aboody from the airport. He'd brought along a female colleague so that Dunia wouldn't be uncomfortable getting into a car with a man she'd never met, even though they'd talked on the phone a few times over the years. He'd promised to shoot me a message when they were headed our way.

I was a bundle of nervous energy, fiddling with my hair and makeup, checking on things in the kitchen, pacing the length of the living room. Then I heard it: *Ding!*

I looked down at my phone. It was Mo: "I've got them! We'll be there in a few minutes!"

My chest tightened and my eyes locked with Tim's. It was time. We'd already decided that Tim and I would go downstairs to meet them without Teeba. We wanted the reunion between Teeba and Dunia to be more private. It would be way too much emotion to display in front of the entire hotel.

"Honey, we'll be right back up," I said to Teeba, a huge lump in my throat.

"Okay, Mom," Teeba said from the kitchen, where she was trying to stay busy helping Mary prepare snacks. To a stranger, it would appear that she was taking this whole thing in stride, staying calm and collected. But I knew she was struggling mightily to control her emotions—excitement, nervousness, and fear of what her mom might think of her.

Tim and I headed into the hall and toward the elevator. He grabbed my hand and held it tight. We rode down in silence, stepped into the hotel lobby, and walked toward the moment that would forever change our lives and Teeba's.

Biting the inside of my cheek from nervous energy, I tried to sit on a low bench by the windows in the hotel lobby, but I just couldn't stay still. I got up and paced the marble floors, back and forth, in front of its wide front windows. Pace, stop, check the driveway. Pace, stop, check. Tim sat quietly in a nearby chair staring out the window. Handsome Emirati men strode by us, dressed in the traditional *kandora*, an ankle-length white cotton robe, with a white headdress known as a *ghutra* held in place by a cord known as an *agal*. The Emirati women dressed in black abayas with black hijabs, and were impeccably made up and perfectly accessorized. The people-watching helped alleviate the excruciating wait a little bit.

Still, it felt like an eternity.

Then we saw it—Mo's black SUV pulled into the hotel drive, and I caught my first glimpse of Dunia's profile through the window of the passenger seat.

"Dunia!"

I burst through the glass lobby doors and ran toward the car, right out into the middle of the street. She turned and saw me and leapt out of the car, even before it had come to a complete stop. She ran toward me, and we met in the middle of the road, hugging each other so hard, clutching each other, kissing each other's cheeks, and sobbing.

"Oh, Dunia, we're finally together! I've waited so long for this," I sobbed into her shoulder. "Dunia, I love you, I love you!"

Through her own tears, Dunia repeated the only words she knew in English over and over: "Barbara, I love you!"

When we finally pulled back from our embrace and looked at each other, I realized I had been holding my breath and was finally able to exhale. And with that exhalation dissolved all of the years of worry that I might not measure up in her eyes when we finally met. Would I be what she expected? Would she approve of me as the woman loving and caring for her daughter? She was so young and pretty; would she look at me as being old? Would she change her mind once she saw me? The years of emotional buildup anticipating this event seeped out of my body and I was able to fully enjoy the moment.

Now I could finally see and touch the woman who had sacrificed so much for her daughter, who had placed her trust in me to raise her. I'd finally connected with her after so many years, and now, here in front of me, was the woman I'd grown to consider my other half. She was lovely, with a warm complexion framed by a bright chartreuse hijab, a joyous smile, and the same piercing dark eyes as Teeba. From that moment, we were no longer two moms to Teeba, divided by geography, language, and culture. We were one.

Behind her, twelve-year-old Fatima, nine-year-old Maryam, and ten-year-old Aboody had climbed out of the car and were standing warily behind their mother. They had started crying, too, probably just because we were and they didn't know what to think. Dunia and I were still holding tightly to each other and didn't want to let go, so we encircled the children in a tight embrace together. Mo came around from the driver's seat, tears in his eyes as well. He was expecting to be there just as a friend, providing some help with transportation and translation, but he was immediately swept up in our outpouring of emotion. I hugged him tight and told him how honored and overjoyed I was to finally meet him. He had been such an integral part of my connection to Teeba's family.

Tim stood beside me, sobbing. I could tell how much he wanted to hug Dunia as well, but this would not be acceptable for a Muslim woman and a strange man. So instead he held out his hand for a simple handshake, which she grasped warmly. Then he knelt down and scooped up the kids in a big embrace.

After standing in the road for five minutes, embracing again and again, it was time to head upstairs. Mo left to park the car, and Tim grabbed the one and only suitcase Dunia had brought for herself and the kids. Dunia was trembling as she clutched my hand tightly, and we walked quickly into the lobby and toward the elevator, the kids trailing behind.

We didn't speak. We didn't need to. No words were necessary to share this moment together.

Dunia and I rode up the elevator in silence, still holding hands. When we reached the twenty-seventh floor and headed down the hallway, Dunia was still shaking beside me. I swiped the keycard, opened the door, and called out to Teeba, who came around the corner from the kitchen and stopped dead in the foyer.

"Teeba! *Habibti!*" Dunia cried, calling her daughter "my love" in Arabic.

She ran toward her daughter—the one who'd left her as a scared, scarred five-year-old and came back to her as a brave, confident young woman.

CHAPTER 31

TEEBA: A MOTHER'S LOVE

Teeba! *Habibti!*"

There she was—my mom Dunia, crying out as she saw me for the first time in nearly ten years, while makeup streamed down her sobbing face.

Just before she and my siblings entered the apartment, I'd been in the kitchen wiping off a glass, pacing back and forth, filled with anxiety, and shouting to Mary in the other room reminding her to take pictures. My biggest concern had been what my mom would think of me, so I'd meticulously selected what makeup I would wear, how I would part my hair, and which shoes I would wear with my blue dress. While everyone else had taken the previous few hours to get some sleep, I was spending every minute I had making sure my mom would think I looked pretty.

Then, all of a sudden, the moment I'd dreamed about was here. I heard the door open and my mom's and dad's voices saying, "Teeba, we're here!" My heart sped up to what felt like a million beats per minute as I stepped around the corner and into the hallway.

But as I faced my mom Dunia, I stood still, afraid to step any closer. Afraid that if I did I'd wake up and realize it was only a dream. Afraid I'd come so close to something I'd prayed about for so long, only to see it disappear.

She stepped closer to me. And closer. Her arms were spread and her eyes were filled with tears. I reached for her—and I finally hugged my mom. The moment I'd dreamed of. Over the years I have always been able to feel Barbara's embrace, and I knew she was an angel just by her warmth and her voice. Now, my months of wondering if my mom would feel the same were over. She was clearly the strongest and most beautiful woman alive, along with my mom Barbara. I could tell just by the way she called me *habibti* and the way she smiled at me. She knew it was hard for me to see her again with so many years between us, and she eased my nerves with just one hug.

I've never been good at outwardly showing my emotions. But I'm not a robot—I have emotions, and at times those emotions feel overwhelming. I suppose my journey has hardened my shell and thickened my skin. In Dubai, my worlds collided. The reunion with my family broke that shell inside me. It's a phenomenon I can't describe—a breakdown of all doubts and disbelief as I looked into the eyes of the woman who gave birth to me.

But the tears didn't come until my family sat beside me on the couch so that my mom Barbara could take a photograph. Fatima was sitting beside me and put her gentle hand on mine. She was innocent and precious, with a smile so graceful. I could not believe this was the same girl who used to catch snakes with me. As I turned to smile at her, she whispered "I love you," in English, and my shell shattered. My eyes filled with tears, and my heart grew heavy with a feeling of regret over not watching her grow up all these years.

Holding each other, we all looked into the camera and smiled. I'd never before felt such a peaceful happiness.

My siblings quickly warmed up to the idea of having another one of "them" around to drink the same water, to tickle, and to share their food. There was plenty of room for us to have our own beds, but that night my mom, siblings, and I all climbed into one king-sized bed together. That's where we all ended up sleeping every night of the trip. Maryam and Aboody would fight over who was going to sleep next to me, so every time he tried to get comfortable she would push him away, which meant he usually ended up being squeezed out to sleep on the ground beside the bed.

I'm not fluent in Arabic, but I knew just enough to understand their stories even when a translator wasn't around. Our favorite topic was our dad. My dad Furat was required at a young age to serve in the army in exchange for a house owned by the government. He had been denied a visa and was not able to join my family on their trip to Dubai. So, my mom and siblings stayed up late at night with me and told me all about him—told me that he loved lamb, like me, and despised milk, like me. They even said he was in love with dancing, like me. They reminded me what an amazing man he is, and as I listened to these stories, it was as if I could smell his cologne and his cigarettes and hear the deep tones of his voice.

I felt so blessed—living there in an apartment with the Iraqi family I'd had to say "goodbye" to, the American family that had said "welcome," and the Perottis, friends who have always said "have faith." My worlds collided. My heart swelled. I said "Thank you, God" every time I woke up next to my mom, every time my sister asked me to pick her up, and every time my brother asked me to race him.

I knew I would be more than heartbroken to see them go, but my deepest wishes and dreams had come true. What more could I ask?

CHAPTER 32

AMER-IRAQI MOMS

By the time we'd recovered from the emotion of the reunion, all of us women looked like raccoons, with mascara dripping down our faces. We cleaned ourselves up, then Pat, Sharon, and Mary came out of their bedroom to meet Dunia and the kids. Mo came up from parking the car, and the party started. We'd strewn snacks across the length of the dining room table, with all kinds of candy for the kids. Teeba put on some music—a playlist she'd created on her iPhone that was a mix of Arabic music and American pop songs.

Then out came the gifts. I'd brought clothes, jewelry, headbands, S'well water bottles, perfumed soaps, and games for each of the kids and Dunia. But also, just for Dunia, I had purchased a beautiful, soft negligee, which I presented to her with a wink. She burst into laughter. I didn't know how to judge her size before meeting her, so to my dismay, it was way too big for her. She assured me she could take it in. We'd also bought her and the girls special necklaces. Each came with a card, which Nazek had translated into Arabic, explaining the symbolism of the pendant. We were all filled with such joy and happiness and laughter that we could have given one another plain empty boxes and they would have been treasures.

Then it was Dunia's turn, and she unzipped the one single suitcase she'd brought for her and all three kids for the entire week. It was as if she'd just opened up Mary Poppins's carpet bag, with triple the amount of stuff crammed in there than would have seemed possible. She pulled out dresses and jewelry for Teeba, and a watch and tie for Tim. She'd brought ties for Pat and Mo, too, and a dress for Mary. For Sharon she produced a necklace that spelled *God* in Arabic. She knew Sharon had vision problems, so as she gave her the necklace, Dunia pointed to her eyes, then to Sharon's, then put a hand on her heart. No translation was needed to hear her message. *I understand you. I feel for you.*

Dunia just kept pulling more and more things out of this seemingly bottomless bag. For me, she had beautiful scarves and two dresses she said were from Furat, and a gorgeous caftan from her. She presented me with a long silver necklace with a turquoise-colored pendant surrounded by rhinestones, which she'd bought nine years prior. She'd intended it as a gift for me when Teeba first arrived in the United States but had forgotten to send it with Amal. She'd kept it all those years, waiting for the opportunity to give it to me in person.

Then, just as I thought I had my emotions in check, Dunia presented me with a chest that looked like a large jewelry box. It was covered in white faux leather with dark bronze hinges and a hook, and it was ornately decorated with white plastic flowers with pearls at the centers, silvery swirls, and bronze nailheads. It was so delicate that I'm certain she had to hand-carry it on the plane.

Dunia looked into my eyes, motioning that I should open it. Inside, the box was lined in red satin fabric with a tiny mirror in the lid. It contained what appeared to be a small bundle of white fabric. I reached in and pulled out a tiny infant-sized shirt, white trimmed with pink and the letters "OK" on the front. Below that was a tiny white bib trimmed in blue with Arabic lettering, tiny bells, and blue beads stitched to the front.

They were Teeba's baby clothes.

A sob caught in my throat. Closing my eyes for the briefest second, I had a vision of Teeba as a baby, with smooth, unscarred skin and a full head of soft black hair, wearing these tiny clothes. My heart broke as I pictured Dunia assembling this gift for me that was so precious, especially when she'd already entrusted me with her most precious possession—her daughter—for so many years.

These are the kinds of things most mothers would keep close to themselves in a treasured spot, where they could hold the soft fabric close to their faces and return to the memories of their babies even long after they'd left home. Yet this extraordinary woman was sharing with me a most prized gift—clothing of Teeba's that she wore prior to the accident, when Yousif was alive and they were a young couple with hopes and dreams of having a big family and raising their children to adulthood. As I held the tiny little clothes, I envisioned Teeba in them. I raised them to my nose to inhale the memory of those days gone by, perhaps even the scent of their home in Diyala. It was as if she were trying to catch me up on the first five years of Teeba's life that I missed, while I tried to do the same from the last nine years that she'd missed.

With Mo translating, Dunia explained to me the significance of this small chest. It was a Koran case, handed down to Dunia from her mother, who had received it from her mother on her wedding day. With each passing down of this treasured chest, where the family's holy Koran was stored, more decorations were added. Dunia received it when she married Furat, and now she was handing it to me to watch over until I could pass it on to Teeba on her wedding day. Dunia and I sobbed, while Teeba stood watching it all with a "when are these two going to stop crying?" look on her face. My breath was caught in my chest, and I felt like I couldn't exhale.

At that moment I truly felt Dunia and I shared the same blood.

Everyone ran off to their respective rooms to try on their new clothes, then returned to the living room to model for the rest of the group. I even tried on Dunia's abaya. We turned up the Arabic music and Dunia, Teeba, and the kids began to dance while everyone laughed and clapped. The kids were glued to Teeba's side. Teeba and Dunia are amazing dancers, gyrating their hips in time to the music. Sharon and I tried to move our bodies the same way, but it was pretty comical. Tim and Pat just sat back and enjoyed the entertainment.

All of us laughed, cried, danced, sang, and cried some more.

After a few hours, we decided it was time to grab some dinner. Before we left, though, Dunia and the kids were thrilled by the opportunity to take showers, since hot running water is available only intermittently in the family's home in the village. They unpacked, cleaned up, and we all headed to the nearby Mall of the Emirates to get some dinner.

As shocking as the opulence of Dubai's malls was to us Americans, I can only imagine how overwhelming it was to Dunia and the kids, coming from a poor rural Iraqi village. The Mall of the Emirates is packed with more than 650 stores—eye-popping jewelry stores, high-end shoe and clothing stores, and wealth on exhibit everywhere you look. People from so many cultures were bustling around, arms weighed down with designer-brand shopping bags. Even though the only skin the Muslim women exposed was that of their hands, feet, and faces, they had flawless makeup, perfectly polished fingernails, and elegant accessories.

I watched the faces of Dunia and the kids to guess at what they thought about all of this opulence, but I could see none of it mattered. The only thing they saw was Teeba. She was their wealth, their jewel, and finally they were together as a family. That was all I saw too. I wouldn't have traded a minute for any of the wealth and jewelry before me.

We made our way to The Cheesecake Factory, which had an extensive menu that included Arabic food, but Dunia made it clear she was having none of it. She wanted Iraqi food, and we wanted to give her what felt most comfortable and familiar. We found a Lebanese restaurant that had better choices for her and the kids, who promptly fell asleep at the table right after eating. All of us were exhausted from the anticipation and emotion of the day, and after dinner we headed back to the apartment to get some sleep.

From that day on, Dunia and I began calling ourselves the Amer-Iraqi Moms, two halves of the same person, bound together forever by our love of Teeba. We bonded so deeply and quickly—I felt like I was with my sister, twin, daughter, and mother, all rolled into one. All the fears and anxiety I'd harbored for months leading up to this trip had vanished, with pure joy taking its place. God had indeed blessed this reunion. I truly felt His Spirit with us, and peace and pure love enveloped us.

The next morning began a whirlwind week. We picked up two new members of our entourage—Rio Altaie, a friend of Nazek's who'd offered to help with translations, and his daughter Malak. An Iraqi living in Dubai, Rio is a grand master of several martial arts disciplines who also hosts his own television program in Dubai. He tagged along with Tim, Teeba, Mary, and Pat to get the kids conservative bathing suits so that they could go in the hotel's rooftop pool, an experience they'd never had before.

Sharon and I took Dunia shopping for clothes, shoes, and anything else she wanted or needed—especially since she'd come with only two outfits for the entire week. We had no translator with us, but she made it clear which outfits she liked. If I held up a blouse or jacket she didn't like, she would scrunch up her face, waggle a finger, and make a "tsk-tsk" noise. We bought her a dress, four blouses, and the first two pairs of jeans she'd ever owned. We also stopped at a fancy grocery store packed with exotic foods and stocked up on ingredients so that Dunia could prepare one of her home-cooked Iraqi meals for us the next day.

Many of our destinations were located in malls, but Dubai's malls aren't like anything you'd see in the United States. The heat in Dubai can be unbearable—with highs around 119 degrees when we were there—so the malls are enormous buildings where, in addition to shopping, tourists can get involved in just about any activity. After we shopped, we met up with the rest of the group at the Dubai Aquarium and Underwater Zoo, located inside another massive Dubai mall and packed with hundreds of species of aquatic animals—including sharks, rays, penguins, and the largest alligator in the world. We took a glass-bottomed boat ride that terrified Teeba's siblings, who thought that surely one of the fish would break through the glass and eat them. The day ended with dinner overlooking the Dubai Fountain, a spectacular water, light, and music display that stands in front of the Burj Khalifa, the world's tallest building at more than 2,700 feet and 160-plus stories.

We tried to take a group selfie in front of the fountains and the Burj Khalifa after dinner, with Rio framing the shot. Imagine trying to get any group of eleven people—including four children—to look in the same direction and smile, then imagine that only half of them could speak English. Over and over Rio shouted "Everyone smile!" and "Look over here!" in English and in Arabic. He ended up taking dozens of photos, but we still never got one where everyone was smiling and looking in the right direction.

But it didn't matter that we never got a perfect shot. Each of them captured the joy and laughter of that first night together.

The next morning Dunia treated us all to Teeba's favorite Iraqi breakfast, which consisted of eggs with potatoes, cheese, and tikka spice, served with oranges and strawberries on the side. After breakfast, while we cleaned up the dishes, Pat packed up the kids with their newly purchased swimsuits and headed up to the rooftop pool. Swimming in a pool, clean and free of crocodiles, was an experience they had been begging for.

They were back in less than an hour, each of them looking like the cat that swallowed the canary—tight-lipped and guilty. It turned out they'd been chased out by the angry, screaming Chinese pool manager who spoke no English. Aboody had pooped in the pool. A typical boy, he'd tried to deny it, but his sister called him out on it.

With no translator around, Pat attempted to use charades to explain to Dunia what had happened. Standing in the middle of the room, half squatting, he started making a motion with his hand to simulate something coming out of his rear end. All of us who knew what had happened were roaring in laughter at this sideshow. But once Dunia figured it out she was mortified, grabbing her son and hustling him off to the shower. We tried not to make it seem like we were laughing at Aboody, though, who thought the entire episode was hilarious. He is a typical high-energy boy who's always looking to play comedian.

Each day came with a new adventure.

Aboody or Maryam were constantly saying in English, "Uncle Pat, Uncle Pat! Papa Tim, Papa Tim! Swim, swim?" and dragging them off to the pool. They didn't know how to swim, but Teeba tried to teach them as they laughed for hours. Mo would pick us up and shuttle us around to activities, but trying to keep all of us together was like herding cats.

Mo joined us in many of our adventures, and it took him by surprise how swept up he became in the emotion of this reunion. He clearly expected to lend a hand with transportation and translation and then go on his way. But he found himself crying right along with us, feeling more and more attached to all of us.

Later, I learned more about the impact our story had on him when I got this message from his mother, Sawsen:

> Mo promised me that you are going to visit me in Houston. Now all my life and happiness is depending on that moment—to meet this honorable family that made me change all my views of the world. Now I know that the world is still good, and you are the raw model of that, my dear Barbara. Give my love to Teeba, please!

On one of the first days, Mo drove us to see the area where he lived, showed us a marina with row after row of beautiful yachts, and then took us to a mall that had tons of kids' games and a food court. Mary, Tim, and Pat watched the little ones while Dunia, Teeba, Sharon, and I went shoe shopping.

Another day we went to the Mall of the Emirates, where the kids went rock climbing, played games, and bowled. Having never bowled before, the idea of staying in your own lane was foreign for Aboody. He thought you could just toss the ball sideways on any lane, and he even threw the ball while the bar was still down and collecting pins.

One of our days together we spent in Abu Dhabi. A tour guide who spoke both Arabic and English took us on the hour-and-a-half drive south along the coast of the Persian Gulf to visit this city, which is the capital of the United Arab Emirates and second in size only to Dubai. There we visited the Falcon Hospital, a facility that would easily rival some children's hospitals in the United States. It's where wealthy Emiratis bring their pet falcons—beloved the way dogs are in the United States—to board them when they travel, get their nails and beaks trimmed, or have their feathers repaired. The falcons wore tiny leather helmets with blindfolds to keep them calm as visitors held and petted them.

Our next stop was the Sheik Zayed Grand Mosque, an enormous structure constructed of glistening white stone rising out of the sand and concrete, looking almost like a mirage in the waves of heat and dust. The eighty-plus domes and minarets and more than a thousand pristine white columns were all topped with gleaming gold, and the polished marble floor of the courtyard was an intricate mosaic of flowers and leaves, all laid on-site by hand. Inside was the world's largest hand-knotted carpet—immense and with no seams—and chandeliers crafted from 24-carat gold and Swarovski crystals, both handmade inside the mosque.

The whole thing was spectacular.

All of us women had to cover our heads and be modestly dressed for our visit to the mosque. But as we checked in, Dunia was stopped by one of the tour guides, who felt her sleeves were too short because they allowed about two inches of her wrist to show. Eventually, they allowed her to proceed.

Dunia and the kids experienced another first that day—the first time they'd ever seen or stepped into the ocean. The beach was just outside the restaurant where we stopped for a late lunch after the mosque, and their eyes lit up when they saw it. The kids ran down to the shore and straight into the water. Dunia followed them, lifted the hem of her dress, and walked right into the water herself, looking back at us with a smile made of pure joy.

Over the week, the personalities of each of Teeba's siblings began to emerge. Aboody was the clown of the group, and we had to keep an especially close eye on him as we paraded around Dubai. He was obsessed by Teeba's camera, constantly running around snapping pictures of everyone. He loved touching everything, no matter where he was. Fatima was quiet, and she clung to Teeba's side. But she blossomed when they danced together, and with each day she allowed herself to be more vulnerable and animated.

Maryam was the only one who'd never met Teeba. Maryam's personality is a lot like Teeba's—more outgoing and playful than Fatima's. This teeny-tiny little girl loved wearing Tim's size-fifteen shoes. They were almost as big as she was tall. More often than not we would find her sitting up on Tim's shoulders, all six feet, four inches in the air. She always had a mischievous sparkle in her eye, and she captured my heart immediately by saying, in English, "I love you, Mama Barbara." She later sent me an audio message through Viber, saying in English: "I love you, Mama Barbara. I miss you tooooooo," dragging out the "too." It made my heart melt.

Watching these children together, I was astounded at how Dunia had been able to raise such happy and polite children amidst the volatile and hostile conditions in Iraq. The amount of wealth and excess in Dubai shocked us, but Dunia and the kids never seemed fazed or envious about the luxuries they saw. They were truly happy and content with what they had, never asking for anything and immersed in the simple things of life.

Like the bathroom. Aboody in particular loved the bathroom—clean water that never ran out, with all kinds of soaps. Every time he went to the restroom, he'd come out having washed his face, hands, and head vigorously. His hair would be wet and slicked back every time. Having hot water was a luxury too; back home in Iraq, there was a small fire in the bathroom they used to heat the water, which was always cold. They'd never used Western toilets, either, and it was scary for Maryam at first. Teeba showed them how to use it, and Maryam would leap back in fear when it flushed. Dependable electricity and modern infrastructure are the kinds of luxuries I've always taken for granted. They did not.

One morning, as we waited for Mo to pick us up for the day's activities, Teeba sat beside Dunia on the living room couch and asked her mother to brush her hair. As the morning sun streamed through the windows on mother and daughter, Dunia carefully brushed Teeba's wig. Dunia's gentle touch began to make Teeba sleepy, so she laid down, put her head in her mother's lap, and pulled a soft blanket over her body. Aboody tucked himself under the blanket at Teeba's feet, and Fatima sat on the floor watching her sister fall asleep, her face just inches from Teeba's.

After Teeba drifted off, Dunia laid aside the hairbrush and began to gently run her fingers along the lines of the remaining scars on Teeba's face, her tears flowing and her grief so evident in every breath. Then she pulled Teeba's wig to the side and ran her fingers over the bumpy cartilage where Teeba's outer ears had been burned off. It was as if she was trying to will away Teeba's scars—to turn back the clock and spare her daughter from years of pain and suffering. She used the tips of her fingers to commit every inch of Teeba's face to memory, crying silently and using her hijab to wipe away her tears.

I felt God's presence in the room so palpably. It was as if He had orchestrated this very moment to allow Dunia some sort of closure. It was a way for her to take all the memories of Teeba's first five years and trace them on top of the last nine years. She could now feel, as well as see, Teeba's progress. She could be reassured that her decision to let Teeba go was the right one, and allow herself the opportunity to forgive herself, to free herself from the guilt she had felt all these years.

I believe this intense emotional release allowed her to breathe again.

The quiet of the apartment was thick with the emotion of this moment. Tim and I watched from the dining room, both of us trying to keep our own tears quiet so as not to break the spell. I tiptoed to the window and pulled the drapes closed to block the blinding sunlight, then left a box of tissues on the table beside Dunia. I snuck off to call Mo and ask him to postpone our pick-up time. After all their years of separation, this wasn't a moment between Teeba and her mother that we could cut short.

Tim and I still cannot speak about it without crying.

Finally, after about an hour and a half, Dunia met my eyes and motioned for me to wake Teeba. I walked to the couch and gently stroked Teeba's shoulder. As her eyes fluttered and opened, she saw both of us and her face lit up, serene and happy. All the guilt and uncertainty wiped clean. I saw her relief that her two mothers were bonded so closely, with no competition—allowing her to let go of her guilt about calling me "mom" in the presence of her birth mother. Here were both women, both mothers who love her unconditionally.

It was another God moment—God opening Dunia's and my minds and hearts to sharing Teeba, loving her and putting only her future at the forefront of our thoughts. As emotionally draining as it was, there was a sense of peace and closure.

We had truly become one Amer-Iraqi Mom.

Every night as the kids played or slept, Dunia and I sat together in the living room with our iPads, attempting to have conversations through Google Translate. As fearful as I had been about coming to Dubai, she revealed she had been just as worried. She had been afraid to meet us, wondering how we would react to her customs. She was unsure of what she would learn about these people who had been raising her daughter for nine years.

"I see my daughter, clean and poised and reserved and confident, and I know that she is in the right place," Dunia told me in one of our rough Google Translate conversations. "I see how Teeba loves you and how you love each other. You are exactly the kind of family I would want to raise my daughter."

One night, trying to convey my devotion to her and my willingness to do anything to protect her, I typed, "I would kill for you" into my iPad. As she read the translation, Dunia began howling with laughter. My sentence had translated to, "I want to kill you." Even when Google Translate failed us or our conversations were a jumble, somehow it didn't matter. There was such immense value in conveying our thoughts and feelings through our actions. We just figured it out.

Over that week we learned more about day-to-day life for Dunia and her family. She continues to struggle with the indifference she's long endured from her in-laws, who still judge her for allowing Teeba to stay in the United States. We'd already witnessed, over and over, the control that the grandparents have over their adult children and grandchildren in Dunia's family. Though Furat approved of the trip to Dubai, they'd had to tell Amal that Dunia and the kids were going to Erbil, Iraq, for a wedding. They'd managed to get the kids to keep the secret too; if Amal found out in advance, she would have insisted on going and trying to bring Teeba back to Iraq. This kind of family dynamic is an archaic tradition that Rio told us later is not frequently found in Iraq anymore, and it was evidence to him how much the conditions in small villages like hers have regressed.

What is so special is Dunia's deep love for Furat. She brought one of his undershirts to slip over her pillow so she could sleep on it and smell him through the nights. She described her feelings for him as being her whole world, her air, her life. My heart ached for her at having Furat away from home for long periods of time in the military—at that time fighting against ISIS—to protect their city and improve life throughout Iraq. She told us he instructed her not to call him sometimes so that the phone wouldn't give away their location. Most times she had to wait for him to communicate with her, and that could be weeks. I couldn't imagine the amount of worry and stress that brought to their household.

Dunia told us about the danger that was part of everyday life in her village. Back in 2014, Fatima and Maryam had been playing in the street with friends when Dunia got a bad feeling and called them into the house. Moments later a bomb went off, killing the other two little girls and blowing out the windows of her house. Another time, the family was preparing for the wedding of Dunia and Furat's niece, and relatives were arriving from all over the region. The night before the wedding, a car bomb exploded, killing or injuring members of the groom's family who were in town for the celebration—including some little girls Maryam had just been playing with the previous day.

Again and again, Mo would tell me that Dunia would say something in Arabic followed by me expressing the same thought in English. When I told him that I look at the moon at night and think of her, Mo said that Dunia had previously shared with him that she did the same thing. Or when I had a migraine and Dunia said she sensed that I was in pain. I've never had that kind of connection with someone.

As Americans, all of us were devastated thinking about the life that Dunia and her children had to return to. But as the week wore on, we saw that our lives were different from hers, but that she wouldn't have been happy in ours. She passionately loves her husband, her family, and her culture. Her belief in God is profound, and she is a humble woman raising wonderful children the best she can. Who was I to judge Dunia's level of happiness without the comforts I am so accustomed to? I was thinking about all the things she didn't have—not the things she does have.

This was the lesson I learned from her.

As the week wore on and we got closer to the moment we would have to say goodbye, our conversations grew more emotional. Dunia poured out her gratitude again and again to Tim and me for everything we had done for Teeba. Just as I do, she sees God's hand on Teeba and the journey she's taken, and she praises God—*alḥamdulillāh*—at the opportunities her daughter has received by growing up in the United States.

On our final night all of the adults in our group agreed to get our emotions about their departure out together, in private, to make the goodbyes easier the next day for the children. We needed to do our best to be strong and hopeful and not break down in front of the kids in the morning. We stayed at the apartment, and Mo brought over pizzas and salads.

The rest of us were continuing our stay in Dubai an extra week to allow us some transition after saying goodbye to Dunia and the kids before returning to America. It would have been too hard to just jump on the plane and come home abruptly.

So we all pitched in to help them get ready to leave. The kids were goofing off in the kitchen while the adults talked about plans to see each other again. We couldn't make exact plans, but we at least needed to talk about possibilities—we couldn't just leave each other with everything open-ended. We spent hours talking, crying, and holding each other, knowing we needed to sleep but not wanting to waste a waking moment. I promised Dunia that this would not be the last time she saw her daughter. We had come too far and waited too long to see each other, and now that we had, we would not let go of her. I, too, needed to be with her. I needed my other half.

I told Dunia I wished I could go back with her to Iraq. Her reaction was swift and emphatic.

"No!" she said in English and Arabic. "And *never* Teeba!"

The next morning everyone was subdued as we helped Dunia get packed up and ready to go. Gone was the laughter and excitement. We adults were biting our lips, trying not to cry, as we headed downstairs to meet Mo. He would drive them to the airport.

I felt especially bad for Tim. My husband is very emotional and sensitive. Tim was crying, and just like when Dunia arrived, I could see how badly he wanted to hug her and reassure her that everything would be okay. And I could tell that Dunia wanted to accept and return that hug, and how difficult it was for her not to show her love and appreciation in a more demonstrative way. While she'd only been able to shake one of his hands when she arrived, by the final day she'd grown comfortable enough with him to stretch both hands out to him and hold them firmly as she said goodbye, looking at him square in the eyes with love and admiration. She'd told Mo earlier in the week that she looked upon Tim as not only Teeba's other father, but also as her own brother.

When that final moment came, Dunia and I held on to each other for dear life. I felt like we were being ripped apart when she turned away to say her goodbyes to Teeba. The weight of those last few moments was suffocating. Aboody, Fatima, and Maryam hugged and kissed and held us all tight, telling each of us in English how much they loved us and would miss us. Over the week the kids had taught Teeba the Arabic word *waead* ("promise"), and the morning of their departure they'd been talking about the future too—dreaming of another visit to the Middle East for Teeba and one day a visit to the United States for them.

"*Waead?*" they asked Teeba, begging for her reassurance that they would see one another again someday.

"Promise," Teeba replied.

CHAPTER 33

DUNIA: ANGELS
ON EARTH

I can wipe away all my life, and I would say I only lived six days, and this was in Dubai. It was the only six days of my life, nothing else. Because these are the best days I ever lived in my life.

I was never born until I saw that day in Dubai. All my sorrows have gone, all my sadness is gone. I was the happiest person ever when I saw Teeba. I saw her as a young, lovely girl. I saw her as wonderful, elegant, tall, and with lovely eyes. I couldn't believe it. That day I was really born. My kids—those were the happiest days in their lives. Still today they dream of going back to Dubai to play and tickle and laugh with their sister.

Little words and statements don't show the tears of joy and happiness when I see my daughter, this beauty with this smile.

Barbara, your love and generosity covered the oceans and the world for me. As I'm fasting, and as I break my fast, the moment I put a drop in my mouth I start praying for you both. I really don't know what I can give you as a gift for what you did for my dear daughter. Then I thought the best thing to give you is my fasting and prayers; you are the most important people I can ever give this gift.

Without you, Barbara, my daughter would not have lived or laughed. Without you I wouldn't have seen the happiness in my daughter's eyes, seeing that Teeba is strong and beautiful and continuing on the right path of education.

You are angels on earth.

All the time my mother and my brother say, "You are a crazy person if you ever let your daughter come back to Iraq. She is in the best place ever in the United States."

Safety is much better now in our village, but there's still no better life. Not yet. The school is not a school. Not yet. There are no schools in this area, just old homes, and they can't have full classes. They have morning and afternoon because there's no school that can hold all the kids. A contractor was supposed to open schools in our area, but he took the money and ran away. But at least it is safe for my kids.

My mother and my brother tell me to ignore what the other people are saying in my village. They say, "Don't listen to them. Your daughter got the best opportunity of her life."

I saw in Dubai how attached Teeba is to both of you and can't live without you. One day when we were eating in a restaurant and Teeba was hungry, your husband split his food and gave it to her. I was even jealous of my daughter that she has this much love and kindness from a father. I was about to get up and kiss him to thank him for his kindness.

Thank God my daughter left Iraq. Thank God, thank God. But I never imagined she would leave me for this long. All the time, I thought she would finish her surgeries in maybe one year or two years, and she would come back. But the days went and the days went, and the nights were colder than the coldest winter night.

They were darker than the darkest nights ever because there were voices of fear. There were screams and there was silence. In every single wail, I could hear the voice of my daughter screaming, "Mom, Mom, where are you?" Day after day.

My pain and my scars were bigger and bigger and bigger, and my heart was hurt. I lost one child, and then I lost the second. But I had no other choice. The first one I lost, but the other one I left for no other choice. Even now people tell me, "She will forget you." I just go to the roof and scream and scream and cry and cry so no one will hear my voice, only God will hear my voice. Maybe He will be merciful to me.

But I know Teeba is seeing me.

Time was not on my side as a mom. It broke me when God took my son and then took away my girl, but in the end I will never ever forget the mom that suffered and sacrificed for a stranger child from a far-distant continent, from a completely different belief and religion, and still brought her into her home. She took her in and hugged her after every surgery, and she prayed with tears that this child will survive all these surgeries and come back to me as a healthy, beautiful child.

I could never forget what Barbara did, and how much she suffered, and the tears she dropped for Teeba and my family.

After I saw Teeba in Dubai, I trust that she is a strong, conservative girl you have raised. Barbara, I could never have been able to raise a girl like you did. I am so proud of her. I am so thankful for you.

CHAPTER 34

TEEBA: ALL PART OF HIS PLAN

M any people say I'm brave. They say I'm strong, and they say I'm courageous. But in reality, I'm just patient. I've been patient since the day the doctors told my family I was severely burned, the day we found out my brother joined the angels in heaven, and the day I moved to America.

I have always found it entertaining when someone stresses about something that is out of their control, only because it is crazy to me that they could ever doubt God's plan for us. Like my mom Barbara, who is afraid to fly on planes, becomes hesitant when traveling anywhere not as developed as America, and stays awake walking around the house in attempts to ease her mind over small matters. I always remind her that we will never be left stranded and unanswered. No matter how often things seem to be hopeless, everything always works out in the end.

It is difficult for me to convey this message, because it is not solid proof of God. It won't make you believe in any superior power if you don't let it. You must live in my shoes to fully understand the millions of events where I have seen God take control. You must watch people around you nearly break down from heartache. You must sit there with me while my head is to the ground saying *alḥamdulillāh* while asking God to take someone's suffering away, and you must be there to watch my prayers be answered as the person I prayed for is now at ease.

God hears us even when we ourselves don't.

God has an answer to every question, but over the years I've realized people are too scared, too lazy, or just unwilling to fold their hands and ask. I am not. I never have been. I have asked God many questions and have received an answer for each one. I once asked God why my skin wasn't immaculate and beautiful like other girls my age. It seemed like I had asked this question to Him over and over again because, obviously, I was aware I was burned. But I didn't understand why the bomb had to leave such permanent and noticeable scars. It seemed like God had simply forgotten to reply to me.

Then, when I was nine or so, I was giving a speech at a fund-raiser that benefited children with other facial disfigurements. As I recited my speech, I began to get goosebumps, because as soon as the audience stood to applaud me, it became evident why the burden of a burned face was placed on me. God wanted my experiences, and the experiences of others He has chosen, to humble more of His people. He wanted it to be proven that with Him anything is possible, and that He uses people like myself, my family, and many others who have suffered to show His grace in each of our lives.

One night, a few years ago, I cried the whole night, whispering to myself: "If it weren't for me, would Yousif be alive?" I sobbed, doubting my right to be exactly where I was. I prayed to God. I distinctly remember saying in my head: *And now a message for Yousif.* So I spoke to Yousif as if he were sitting a foot away from me. I updated him on how our siblings were doing in school, and I apologized because I felt that he would still be alive if I were not in the taxi that day. I asked him, "Will I ever see you again?" But I never got an answer.

Then, about two months later, I was standing in line with my mom Barbara at Nazek's daughter's wedding shower. In the food line behind us was a cute little Arab boy who kept disobeying his mother when she told him to stay still, running around her in circles. My mom asked his name and how old he was.

"His name is Yousif," the mother said with a smile. "He's three years old."

My heart felt like it stopped for an entire minute. I realized God had answered me. Yousif is a sweet, innocent, and free child that prevails in the hearts of many, just like the little boy that day. I'm always reminded of my brother who passed away when I see young children running around without a care. I don't remember my brother much, just that he loved marbles. But my mom Dunia said the day my brother died, not only did she lose her son, but I lost my best friend. I feel as if I know him to the core, and one day when we meet again, maybe I will find out I already know everything I need to know about him.

Reconnecting with my family was an awakening that also helped me reconnect with my faith. I've always believed in God and in prayer, but seeing my mom and my siblings again made me want to learn more about the heritage of my birthplace. I have seen how faith got my family through so many years of hardship in Iraq, and I desire to feel that same connection and make it part of my everyday life.

My longest ongoing prayer was to see my mom Dunia again. Now I feel so close to her even when we are separated. She texts me to say she doesn't feel well because she has a sense that I'm tired, sick, or hungry. It's like she can read my mind from the other side of the world. She knows what I want when I don't know myself.

My mom in Iraq made me realize that family does not mean you have to be within arms-length distance. It just means your hearts have to be bonded together. My mom in America taught me that family doesn't always mean you are related by blood, but rather with love. So I prayed to have my big, multicultural family in one room. Just one more hug from my mom. Just once to see my siblings and to introduce them to the parents who have raised me in America.

With the help of God, my American family made these prayers come true in Dúbai.

I have been through a lot, and that might be an understatement. But what is so great about experiencing the best of the best and the worst of the worst is all the lessons you get to learn. Through everything I have endured, I have learned the value of a human life and the cost of it.

Over the years, I have also learned there are people in this world who want to bring you down. There are people in this world who want to see you cry. There are even people in this world that hate you because of the blessings you have been given. I have learned I am a lucky girl. I know I have scars on my face, hands, head, and legs, but I am luckier than the pretty girl that sits in the front of my class. Sure, she has blond, beautiful hair that actually grows from the roots of her head; she has perfect, flawless skin; and she gets to hug the mom who gave birth to her every night. But someone once told me something so simple, yet I'd never realized it before: "Tee, you gotta be more than just pretty."

So yes, being pretty is nice. Being a nice person is even better. But, having an effect on people is what I strive for. In my life, I want people to remember me as the miracle that walked through the door and stayed humble. I don't care if I don't look like a CoverGirl model. I don't care if *Vogue* says pretty skin is the best skin. I don't care if *Seventeen* magazine thinks blond hair will make you more popular. At the end of the day, when I apologize to God for my hostile attitude to that one classmate or thank Him for the extra five minutes of sleep, I only care what He hears. I only care what He thinks of me. He is the only one who has the right to say someone is of lesser worth than someone else. He didn't appoint mean girls or rude adults to make that decision.

I didn't choose to be born into a traditional family in the Middle East. I didn't choose to be burned in a bomb. And I didn't choose to leave my home at five years old. But if I were given the choice today, I wouldn't change one thing. Everything happens for a reason. It's your choice how you are going to deal with it. For me, it was praying and surrounding myself with wonderful people.

I have shared my story in speeches before, and nothing is more rewarding than watching the awe in my audience's faces when I make them realize something they had never understood before. To put the idea of "worth" and "value" in perspective, I always pull out a twenty-dollar bill and ask the crowd: "Do you want this money?" to which they always reply, "Yes!"

"What if I crumpled it or stomped on it?" I say. "Do you still want it?"

"Yes!" they always reply.

I crumple the bill up in my hand. "But don't you notice that it's damaged?"

"Yes!"

"But why? Didn't it lose its value already? It looks completely different."

Silence.

"See, even with all this piece of paper has endured, it has kept its value and worth. And after nineteen painful surgeries, I have come to understand I haven't lost my worth either. This money is still money. This person, me, is still a person."

I wish I could promise a happily-ever-after ending. But the truth is, my story is not over yet. I have not completed the mission I was sent to accomplish. I still have a long way to go to impact and inspire people the way I hope to. I have not persuaded enough people to live and let live, and I especially haven't convinced all my friends there are bigger problems in this world than the little things they worry about every day. I didn't always like the media attention I got and the television cameras in my face as I was growing up. But when the camera goes on, I have to remember that this isn't really about me. It's about sharing my story in a way that helps people.

I have more items to check off my checklist, and I have more adventures to discover. Throughout it all, I will continue to thank God for the amazing people in my life, like my families, friends, and extended family.

I will thank Him for my thick skin and for my endless opportunities that have allowed me to meet honorable people like Vice President Mike Pence; the Iraqi ambassador to the United States, Dr. Fareed Yasseen; the former Iraqi ambassador to the United Nations, Mohamed Ali Alhakim; as well as Senator Rob Portman, Ohio Governor Mike DeWine, and US congressman Jim Renacci.

But hear me loud and clear—I will continue to work to make this world understand how suffering, separation, and loss are not always bad things. They can be turned around, flipped inside out, reversed, and transformed into something worth the pain.

Mark my words—I will be coming back to you to tell you the end of my happily-ever-after story. And I will make it count.

EPILOGUE

After so many years of fighting to bring Teeba here and keep her here, I now face the heartache of preparing myself to let her go. When this book is published, she will be seventeen and in tenth grade. College is waiting just around the corner. It frightens me.

I'm sixty-five years old. Tim is seventy-six. I worry, as does Tim, that we won't be here to see Teeba graduate from college or to walk her down the aisle at her wedding. I'm afraid we won't be here to help when she has her first child or to watch her finish medical school.

By growing up in the United States, Teeba has been able to escape so many of the dangers and challenges that Dunia and Furat feared for her in Iraq. She has received an education and the medical treatment she desperately needed. If she had never received treatment, her pain and disfigurement would have only gotten worse. As she grew, her scarred skin would have become even more constricted and painful, and she would have had more and more difficulty moving her neck and opening her mouth.

Teeba will never look completely "normal"; she will always experience some stares from strangers at times. But for the most part, no one seems to notice anything different about her—not about her appearance, anyway. She is confident and well liked at school. She has a close group of friends, even some with whom she feels comfortable enough to take off her wig. She has established herself as a leader among her peers, and she tries her very best to avoid all gossip and criticism of others.

Today, Teeba is beautiful inside and out. As her skin has been gradually replaced and this gorgeous butterfly has emerged from the chrysalis, Teeba has grown into her own as a well-rounded, smart, and savvy young woman. She overcame the struggles with her appearance over the years by developing a huge personality with a great sense of humor, confidence, and a rare intuition about others. She knows when others are being disingenuous, and she values authenticity.

We have seen Teeba's faith in God grow in ways beyond what we could have imagined for a teenager. She has a heightened sensitivity to anyone who is sad, hurting, or disabled. She defends those who cannot defend themselves, and she confronts people who criticize or ridicule others. Teeba came to us as a five-year-old Muslim child and spent much of her childhood living in a Christian home. But as she's grown and reunited with her mother Dunia, she's reconnected to her Iraqi heritage. Teeba is acutely aware of the gifts she has been given by God, and she strives to make Him proud by trying to do what's right.

Teeba has high aspirations for herself: she plans to become a pediatric anesthesiologist, hoping to help other children who feel scared and alone before a surgery, as she did. She hopes that someday she'll be able to return to Iraq to provide medical care to children through an organization like Doctors Without Borders, and she would like to see a free clinic opened up in Iraq. Maybe even in Diyala Province. Tim and I long to be here to see her achieve those dreams. Each of the amazing people she's met over the years has opened up new doors to her future, such as internship opportunities she's been offered at the Iraqi Embassy and the Permanent Mission to Iraq at the United Nations.

To date, Teeba has endured nineteen surgeries and is taking a break from treatment. When she resumes, reconstructing her ears will be the next step. The burns destroyed most of her outer ear and lobes, and it will require at least another three surgeries per ear to reconstruct them, using cartilage taken from her ribs and progressing only one ear at a time. She continues to have laser treatments to soften the remaining scars and discoloration on her face and hands.

But what pains Teeba most is not having hair. Because of the nature of her injuries, she has few options for treatment short of a scalp transplant, which is experimental at this point, too risky, and would require the use of antirejection medications for the rest of her life. I keep hoping and praying that a new and safer procedure will surface. We always consult with Dunia when considering future medical treatments, and she agrees that scalp transplantation is not a viable option yet.

As a legal permanent resident with a green card, Teeba will be able to stay in the United States and can become a naturalized citizen when she turns eighteen. She'll be able to travel freely, and hopefully that will mean many more trips to see her Iraqi family. She hopes that someday she might be able to visit her homeland in more peaceful times.

For my part, I still struggle to allow myself to be truly joyous with Teeba, knowing how intensely Dunia is missing her daughter on the other side of the world. Teeba's milestones are both spectacular and bittersweet, as the piece of me that is intertwined with Dunia feels her sorrow and guilt. I have spent years going back and forth between these emotions— loving and cherishing my time with Teeba until guilt creeps in over the many years that her parents have lost with her. Mo's mother, Sawsen, reassures me that without Tim and me, Dunia might have had to bury two children instead of one. Even though Dunia constantly reassures us, I still hold that little broken piece in me.

I hold it for her.

I cannot imagine my life without Dunia. We're planning now for how we can see her and Teeba's siblings again—and hopefully meet Furat. I am still in awe of how attached Dunia and I have become. We always seem to connect at the times when the other needs it most. An eye specialist finally determined that her vision impairments were the result of severe stress, and she has since fully regained her sight. She somehow knows when something is bothering me, like a migraine. Dunia is young enough to be my daughter, but she is also my sister, my best friend, and the mother of my daughter. We love Teeba's family very deeply and think of them as our family. I worry every day when I read about a suicide bombing or other terrorist attack. I can't sleep until I know everyone is okay.

I keep the Koran case, with Teeba's baby clothes still in it, displayed prominently in a glass cabinet in my kitchen, right next to the Lenox china cross-shaped box with the "God Loves You" golf marker inside. I look at it often, remembering Dunia carefully carrying it all the way from Baghdad to Dubai, and picturing myself giving it to Teeba on her wedding day. For Dunia, I made a coffee-table book of our Dubai trip with a picture of Yousif on the back cover. Over the years I have sent her Teeba's school pictures, schoolwork, baby teeth, and even a big soft blanket with Teeba's face all over it.

Dunia once asked us if, should anything happen to her, we would consider taking the other children so they would have the opportunities America has to offer. Without hesitation Tim and I agreed. Even at our ages, there is no doubt they will forever have a home with us and with their sister.

Teeba has found the balance between her two worlds and is reinforced by the love and support of two moms and two dads. That's more than anyone could ask for—a love that is without jealousy, competition, or judgment. It's truly pure, like God's love for us. I've wished so many times that Tim and I were thirty years younger during this journey. We need another lifetime to relish the joy we have and to be able to see Teeba's future come to life. I am hopeful that when I stand before God, I will hear those precious words, "Well done, my good and faithful servant," and that He will allow me to be Teeba's guardian angel.

My husband has certainly earned his wings. His patience, commitment, and love for this little girl brings tears to my eyes. Tim loves his birth children dearly, and it is incredible to me how he allowed his heart to embrace and accept a fourth, very young child with some severe medical needs in his later years of life. He is wild about Teeba and is in awe of her accomplishments through all the challenges. This journey has brought another dimension to our marriage, bringing out the best in us as partners. We've navigated through tremendous emotional ups and downs to create a brilliant future for Teeba. He is like a Boy Scout—loyal, dependable, and trustworthy. Plus he's proven himself highly skilled at helping with math homework and sorting out the facts in every teenage-girl drama.

We also have the opportunity to advocate for other Iraqi children who have experienced injuries and tragedies in their homeland through the Iraqi Children Foundation (ICF). Seeing the way years of war and terror-ism have impacted her family and friends, Teeba's resolve to take action has been strengthened. She knows the advantages of living in America and how truly lucky and blessed she is.

I recently joined the board of the ICF on Mo's invitation, and Teeba is an honorary youth ambassador. It's given her the opportunity to meet the Iraqi ambassador to the United States, Dr. Fareed Yasseen, as well as other Iraqi children who have experienced injuries far worse than her own— kids like Humoody, who was shot in the face when he was two years old by an extremist group, and A'Ala, who was abandoned in the streets of Baghdad as a child because he has cerebral palsy.

I pray that my work will touch the lives of Teeba's extended family members and friends in Iraq.

I started this journey with one simple thought: *I can get this little girl a wig.* I never imagined it would have been the beginning of a new family, one built here with Teeba and one that has united us with her family on the other side of the world. Through the days upon days spent in hos-pitals, the fears that she might be taken away, the costs of doctors and schools, I have never regretted one minute of my life with Teeba. Not one second. Not a thing.

I AM BRAVE AND LOYAL

I am brave and loyal
I wonder when my dad will come back from war
I hear an encouraging voice in my head
I see people working together
I want to see the good in people

I am brave and loyal
I pretend I can fly
I feel the wind blow past me
I touch the clouds in Heaven
I worry that world peace doesn't exist
I cry when I think about my family in danger

I am brave and loyal
I understand no one is perfect
I say everybody gets a second chance
I dream about being successful
I try to be a caring friend
I hope to make a difference in the world
I am brave and loyal

—Teeba Furate Marlowe, Grade 6
A Celebration of Poets, Grades K-8, Spring 2015

233

ACKNOWLEDGMENTS

Dunia and I had a long, emotional conversation about *A Brave Face*. She has specifically requested that certain people be acknowledged for their generosity, kindness, and support to Teeba. I am honored to do that for her and certainly echo those sentiments. So, from Teeba's two mothers and two fathers, we say . . .

An abundance of gratitude from the depths of our hearts and souls to Dr. Arun Gosain, his surgical team and staff, and of course University Hospitals Rainbow Babies & Children's Hospital in Cleveland, Ohio. Your extreme generosity and willingness to give Teeba a chance for a new life is unmeasurable. Thank you to Dr. Avroy Fanaroff for setting the plan in motion. All of you have rescued her from a lifetime of second glances and judgments. You did indeed push our little caterpillar into a beautiful butterfly. She is soaring to new heights because of all of you, and especially because of Dr. Gosain's gifted hands and beautiful spirit. We would like to acknowledge Lurie Children's Hospital in Chicago, Illinois, where Dr. Gosain is currently practicing, for their role in Teeba's transformation as well. God bless you all.

Thank you to Nazek, Sawsen, and Leila for bridging the language barrier and helping to keep the lines of communication open. During those very difficult times, it was a relief for Dunia and me to be able to communicate with each other mother-to-mother as well as sister-to-sister, and to be able to get to know each other on a more personal level. Nazek, your audio recordings of Dunia's messages brought life to her written stories and gave me great solace; your translations of my messages to Dunia brought her that same comfort. We treasure all the times we were able to make connections on FaceTime as well.

Education is paramount to a foundation for a promising future. We thank and applaud Tina Turk and The Goddard School for taking a chance on Teeba when Mama Barbara didn't know where to turn. We thank Andrews Osborne Academy, Notre Dame Elementary School, Notre Dame Cathedral Latin High School, and Gilmour Academy for educating our daughter and instilling the wisdom and desire for the power of knowledge that will propel her in the pursuit of her goal of becoming a pediatric anesthesiologist.

Heartfelt gratitude to the Khudairi family, especially Mohammed "Mo" Khudairi. Your willingness to help two families on opposite sides of the world, whom you yourself didn't get to meet until nine years later in Dubai, has brought two families together—all for the love of one little girl, our Teeba. Your generosity and gracious spirit gave our families the path in which to send and receive gifts. Best of all for Mama Barbara was to be able to give Mama Dunia an iPad that catapulted our worlds together and created an impenetrable bond. The two moms are now never more than a click away from each other. You and your staff at your Baghdad office went above and beyond by delivering packages directly to Dunia's house. You have been a lifeline for our families. And for me, Mama Barbara, to meet the rest of the Khudairi clan has been a real God send. You have all embraced Teeba and supported our journey with your love and encouragement. Sawsen, Mo's mother, thank you for being a friend, for translating, for being a confidante, and for holding us all so close to your heart. I'm very happy you made me an honorary Iraqi! I'm honored to be on the board of the Iraqi Children Foundation working alongside Teeba in her role as Honorary Youth Ambassador. It is a privilege to serve on the board of this extraordinary organization alongside extraordinary people (www.iraqichildren.org).

ACKNOWLEDGMENTS

And from me, Mama Barbara, thank you to my girlfriends for always being on call for those last-minute "family meetings," and for being a shoulder to cry on when we felt tormented and isolated throughout all those surgeries and subsequent recoveries. Thank you for those random neck massages and helping us to sort out next steps, keeping our emotions in check, and stopping us from the constant stream of second-guessing. I couldn't have done it without you and Maria's turkey sandwiches.

Mama Dunia would like to acknowledge our precious little Maltese, Phantom, who for the remainder of his days, at sixteen years old, didn't want to be bothered with this little girl and couldn't figure out how his life became caught up with this little Iraqi whirling dervish. He was in the original picture that Mama Barbara sent to introduce our family to Teeba. Mama Dunia still treasures that photograph today.

To our family members who made sure Teeba was always included, making her feel accepted, loved, and assuring her that she did indeed have family here as well as in Iraq. Thank you for the comfort you provided to Tim and me, knowing she wouldn't be alone. Thank you to my mom's sister Arlene, whom we call "Kiki," for being Teeba's "Bibi" and teaching her to make the crispy potatoes that she still loves today. I know my mother would've adored her.

To Dworken & Bernstein Co., L.P.A., for your sound advice in helping us with all our concerns and issues from the moment Tim and I stepped into the office as clients, to me then becoming an employee. Thank you for your generosity to Teeba's well-being throughout the years. And to Kim Alabasi, our immigration attorney, we so appreciate the hard work and commitment in making sure we navigated through all the mounds of paperwork thoroughly and especially for allaying my worst fears.

Pat, Sharon, and Mary Grace Perotti. You have been a source of guidance and craziness for "Sasquatch," also known as "Little Teeba." Thanks for all the laughs—especially when we needed the levity. There are no words that can express our appreciation for your encouragement and love. I am especially grateful to you for talking me off the ledge multiple times. Thank you for looking out for our little girl—that comes from Dunia and Teeba's siblings as well. They look to you as family, as do we.

To Elissa and Gary Okin for providing a peaceful and beautiful sanctuary for Jennifer Keirn and me to write—and for me specifically to reflect on our journey and have a good cry in such a tranquil and peaceful setting.

Thank you to Judge Bartolotta and the late Judge Klammer for caring. We are very grateful for your scrutiny and your willingness to dig deep into our circumstances, and for allowing Teeba an opportunity to make a difference in our lives and in our community.

To our late beloved Huda. Thank you to you and your husband, Steve Sosebee, from the PCRF. Without you none of this would have happened. You took a chance on us and believed in our intentions. I certainly valued your efforts, your time, and especially your patience with me specifically. I know it wasn't easy walking me through the political waters and having to reassure me regularly to breathe, be patient, and be vigilant. What a wonderful legacy you have left behind, not only the Huda Al Masri Pediatric Cancer Department in Beit Jala Hospital, but the ongoing work Steve continues to do helping children all over the Middle East get the medical attention they so deserve. You would be so proud of your daughters, Deema and Jenna. The Palestine Children's Relief Fund continues to serve hundreds and hundreds of innocents. God bless you (www.pcrf.net).

To Jennifer Keirn, for treating our story with such respect and honor. From the first article you wrote about us for a feature story in *Cleveland Magazine* in 2010, I knew you were a woman of great faith and talent. Thanks for being our "general contractor" and helping me navigate through the memories and endless tears. I couldn't have done it without you. And a special thank you to your husband, Jesse, and your sons, Jaden and Alex. There were many late nights and weekends you spent working on *A Brave Face* and being apart from them. I'd like to acknowledge your family for their patience and support of you. We look to celebrate continued success with the Keirn family!

ACKNOWLEDGMENTS

Thank you Robert Guinsler from Sterling Lord Literary for remembering our story from the early years and seeing the potential. We are grateful for your commitment to our journey.

And to Megan Dobson and Sam O'Neal from W Publishing at HarperCollins. What can I say! Thank you for taking a chance on us and for allowing me to give God the full credit for so many of the miracles that happened along the way. We feel our story is in safe hands. Our experience with you has been so effortless, and we are so beyond proud to have you as our publisher.

To Teeba's father Furat, who set the ball in motion when he agreed to make that treacherous trip to Baghdad to meet James Palmer and share his daughter's story. We all owe him a great debt of gratitude for his courage and persistence.

And Mama Barbara must save the best for last! To my husband, Tim, thank you is not enough for what you have done and continue to do. Your unwavering support from the day I first saw that newspaper article to where we are today is nothing short of miraculous. You are my angel on earth. You are truly one-in-a-million and I can't fathom being on this journey without you. Papa Tim, you are the most selfless and generous man. Teeba and I love you more than you can even imagine. As I have always said, I hope Teeba marries a man just like you one day—she will be truly blessed.

ABOUT THE AUTHORS

BARBARA MARLOWE is Marketing and Public Relations Director for the law firm of Dworken & Bernstein Co., L.P.A., in northeast Ohio. She has served on several boards for nonprofits and is currently a member of the University Hospitals Rainbow Babies & Children's Leadership Council and Dogs Unlimited Rescue; she is also president of the Iraqi Children's Foundation. Until Teeba's arrival, Barbara was an avid golfer and loved to play in tournaments. She hopes to return to her favorite sport one day very soon. Barbara and her husband, Tim, live in an eastern suburb of Cleveland along with Teeba and their dog Becca.

TEEBA FURAT MARLOWE is a sophomore in high school at Gilmour Academy. She is dedicated to her studies and focused on her future as a pediatric anesthesiologist. She hopes to one day volunteer with Doctors Without Borders. Teeba is an accomplished dancer in various styles of dance and has a talent for creating and editing videos. She is also a gifted public speaker and skilled speech writer. Teeba serves as Honorary Youth Ambassador for the Iraqi Children's Foundation. She does an amazing job of balancing two mothers and two fathers!

JENNIFER KEIRN is an award-winning writer and author whose work has appeared in dozens of publications including *Cleveland Magazine, Ohio*

Magazine, and *Lake Erie Living.* She also frequently writes for major healthcare organizations, educational institutions, and companies of all sizes. A graduate of the Scripps School of Journalism at Ohio University, Jennifer lives outside of Cleveland, Ohio, with her husband and two sons.

PRAISE FOR *A BRAVE FACE*

"Barbara and Teeba's story draws you in and doesn't let go—a truly unbelievable story of hope, kindness, and inspiration. *A Brave Face* is a touching tribute to inner strength and perseverance while redefining the true meaning of 'family' along the way."

—JACK HANNA, Director Emeritus, Columbus Zoo and Aquarium

"The life of a young girl forever changed by a desire to do right has led to a courageous journey for all, reminding us of what happens when good people choose a path that can have great impact."

—RON HAVIV, Photojournalist, Photographer, Cofounder of VII Agency

"I've followed this story for years as it developed, but in *A Brave Face*, I learned the real story of an American family, a child badly injured in war-torn Iraq, and the mercy, goodness, and impact that happens when people step up and step out in love, compassion, and conviction. As you race ahead to read this unfolding human drama, you'll be amazed at how an entire community rallies to support and secure resources to bring this little girl to Cleveland on this life-changing journey. Against our nation's current social discourse of conflict, hatred, and fear, this is a bright ray of hope for what can happen when the human spirit takes over."

—HOWARD L. LEWIS, Founder and Chairman Emeritus,
Family Heritage Life Insurance Company of America

"*A Brave Face* shares a true and sincere example of how humanity is capable of embracing differences to focus on love, tolerance, and compassion. Here are just a few of the many gifts this book will provide to you: a beautiful presentation of human love in its purest form, inspiration for what can be, and a deep hope for our global future. Through these pages, we see a pathway for sincere peace in our world—one compassionate step at a time."

—DENISE GOTTFRIED, Board Member for the
American Society of Plastic Surgeons, President and
CEO of TekTeam Medical Industry Consultants

"Now, when we seem to need it more than ever, comes a story that rekindles our faith in humanity while simultaneously igniting a spirit of courage. Teeba Furat Marlowe, so much more than *A Brave Face*, symbolizes the strength and determination of an entire culture. Barbara Marlowe, through her amazing journey, embodies what is best about people: the selfless acts of compassion and love that often define our life's purpose."

—THOMAS F. PATTON, Ohio State Representative, Majority Whip

"Teeba's journey reminds us that we need not be present in the horrific details of trauma to experience its gift when impacted with healing. Teeba's story pierces across the hearts and waters of humanity. This story of courage and sacrifice has cemented the hearts of three women: one who gave birth, one who held her hand in courage, and Teeba herself."

—LESIA S. CARTELLI, Founder of Angel Faces, Author of *Heart of Fire*

"Teeba is an inspiration to all of us. Stories of hope and courage are revealed every day in the children who come to University Hospitals Rainbow Babies and Children's Hospital for their care, and Teeba is among the most courageous I have known. It has been an honor to be part of Teeba's journey as our physicians, nurses, and community of caregivers at Rainbow have been inspired every step of the way. Her strength and courage through extraordinary circumstances make her story worth telling."

—THOMAS F. ZENTY III, President and CEO, University Hospitals Health System, Cleveland, Ohio